Derek C. Hutchinson

ESKIA ROLLING

THIRD EDITION

With illustrations by the author

**Approved by the British Canoe Union
and the American Canoe Association**

The
Globe
Pequot
Press

A & C Black • London

TO FIONA

my daughter, whose willing determination under my early attempts at coaching
made her a successful Hand-Roller when she was only fourteen.
She is now a married lady and has put away such childish things.

Published by:
A & C Black (Publishers) Limited
35 Bedford Row
London WC1R 4JH, England

The Globe Pequot Press
6 Business Park Road
P.O. Box 833
Old Saybrook, Connecticut 06475-0833

Library of Congress Cataloging-in-Publication Data

Hutchinson, Derek C.
      Eskimo rolling / Derek C. Hutchinson ; with illustrations by the author. -- 3rd ed.
         p.   cm.
      Includes index.
      ISBN 0-7627-0451-9
      1. Kayaking--Safety measures.   2. Survival skills.   I. Title.
   GV784.55.H88   1999
   797.1'224'0287--dc21   99-28696
                                                                    CIP

Acknowledgements
Cover photograph courtesy of Derek C. Hutchinson. All other photographs reproduced as
individually credited. Line drawings by Derek C. Hutchinson. Page design by Judith Gordon.
Cover design by Adam Schwartzman.

Typeset in 11/13 Janson
Printed and bound in Great Britain by Biddles Ltd,
Guildford and Kings Lynn

Contents

Anecdotes

Foreword to the First Edition

Many readers will, I am sure, like me, identify with the embarrassing or unnerving moments which contributors have laid bare within these pages for us to chuckle at or to shake our heads over.

Derek Hutchinson's collection of anecdotes reflects the varying 'state of the art' of Eskimo rolling since the early 1960s. These accounts of rolling mis-adventures, provided by a cross-section of famous and 'infamous' paddlers, are interspersed with explanations of a wide variety of rolling techniques. The source of these techniques lies in the knowledge and ability of the Inuit peoples of past centuries.

It is humbling to realise that the skill of 'hand rolling' a kayak was not unknown in Greenland some 200 years ago, but was only discovered in Britain in about 1966. The ability to perform an Eskimo Roll has, within a generation, moved from being a 'party trick' to being an absolute essential in the severe water conditions – both rapid rivers and the sea – commonly paddled today.

This book, written by a major canoeing writer and personality, adds to our understanding of Eskimo rolling and to Derek's reputation as an authority on kayaks and kayaking.

GEOFF GOOD
DIRECTOR OF COACHING, BRITISH CANOE UNION

I believe that Derek Hutchinson's book on Eskimo rolling will become the bible on this subject for both river and sea coastal paddlers. Instructors, students and seasoned paddlers will find quality advice within its covers. It will inspire us all to improve our skills with the paddle.

CHARLES SUTHERLAND
CHAIRMAN, NATIONAL SEA KAYAKING COMMITTEE
AMERICAN CANOE ASSOCIATION

'By the way, Derek, did I ever tell you about when Alan and I were trying to learn the Put-Across Roll? There was nobody to teach us – no one else knew how to do it. We had this brilliant idea of tying ourselves to the under-side of the dining-table.' 'Sounds hilarious – did it work?' 'Not bad – except it cut off the blood supply to my legs!'

TELEPHONE CONVERSATION WITH CHRIS HARE

You cannot rank as an expert kaiak-man [sic] until you have mastered the art of righting yourself after capsizing. To do this, you seize one end of the paddle in your hand, and with the other hand grasp the shaft as near the middle as possible; then you place it along the side of the kayak with its free end pointing forwards towards the bow; and thereupon, pushing the end of the paddle sharply out to the side, and bending your body well forward towards the deck, you raise yourself by a strong circular sweep of the paddle. If you do not come right up, a second stroke may be necessary.

NANSEN, *Eskimo Life*, pp. 52–3

A thorough kaiak-man [sic] can also right himself without an oar by help of his throwing-stick, or even without it, by means of one arm. The height of accomplishment is reached when he does not even need to use the flat of his hand, but can clench it; and to show that he really does so, I have seen a man take a stone in his clenched hand before capsizing, and come up with it still in his grasp.

NANSEN, *Eskimo Life*, p. 53

Foreword to the Second Edition

The self-rescue technique of righting a capsized kayak without assistance was developed centuries ago by native kayakers in northern waters. These people used kayaks as a swift and silent means of closing within harpooning range of swimming quarry. Native kayakers ran the risk of capsizing in cold water, especially when approaching a large wounded seal or walrus. Their best hope of surviving was to stay in the capsized kayak, because the sea was sometimes below the freezing temperature of fresh water. This led to the self-rescue manoeuvre that recreational kayakers know as the Eskimo Roll.

One of the rolling methods used by Bering Sea kayakers was to roll up by extending the arms from inside the capsized kayak and manipulating the paddle. Other Alaskans learned to save themselves by sticking the paddle up in the air beside the kayak and swinging it downwards to right themselves. But it was in Greenland that kayak rolling reached its highest development, partly because their efficient but risky hunting techniques could lead to accidental capsizes, but also because the solid ice cap there feeds glaciers that calve icebergs larger than those found elsewhere in northern waters. Thus Greenland kayakers might be capsized from the huge waves created when an iceberg calved or a floating iceberg capsized suddenly. Some of these waves could be large enough to flip a kayak end-over-end. The Greenlanders' highly specialised repertoire of kayak manoeuvres probably developed from basic rolling skills brought by their ancestors from the western arctic about 800 years ago.

Kayaking exhibitions given in Denmark and Holland by captured Greenlanders in the early 1600s probably included rolling demonstrations. Ten methods of rolling a kayak were described in 1767 by David Crantz in his *History of Greenland*. Yet it was not until the 1920s that recreational kayakers began to show much interest in learning the manoeuvre.

In 1927 a recreational kayaker named Edi Hans Pawlata taught himself a kayak roll by a modified version of the standard Greenland Roll. Pawlata, pronounced PAVH-LAH-TUH, proudly recorded the date that he achieved success (31 July 1927) in his book *Kip, Kip, Hurra!* (Tipover, Tipover, Hurrah!), which was published in 1928 in Austria. Anyone who has struggled to teach themselves to roll can empathise with the elation that he felt on that occasion! Pawlata was not the first outsider to learn to roll, but he was the first to popularise it among recreational paddlers, who know his method as the Pawlata Roll.

In the early 1930s, two British expeditions went to East Greenland, and most of the members learned to kayak. Gino Watkins, the organizer and leader, became an expert, but he lost his life in a kayaking accident on the second expedition. The two expeditions are described in the books *Northern Lights* and *Watkins' Last Expedition*, both by F. Spencer Chapman.

A Cambridge student named James Moore followed these expeditions with great interest. He built a replica of an East Greenland kayak and met with expedition members after they returned. They helped stimulate the interest in advanced sea kayaking that has continued in England to this day.

Recreational kayaking today has basically become polarised into two main branches. On the one hand is the white-water group, which has a wide following in central and eastern Europe. On the other hand is the sea kayaking group, with its following in the United Kingdom and northern Europe.

Self-rescue technique in white-water rivers is not the same as it is at sea. In most rivers the capsize victim is near shore and faces hazards such as submerged rocks and tree branches, and a current that carries a capsized kayaker into them. It is therefore prudent for a white-water capsize victim to roll up quickly, or bail out of the kayak if two or three rolling attempts fail. Then they can remain on their back, facing downstream, as they work their way toward shore using the current. The urgency of rolling up quickly has made the Screw Roll popular among white-water paddlers because the paddle does not need to be extended. This saves time and enables the kayaker to continue paddling immediately after the roll. Sea kayakers, on the other hand, are farther from shore, which often translates into more time immersed in cold water. A major danger to a capsized sea kayaker is exposure. Getting out of a kayak into cold water can quickly sap the strength of an expert swimmer, which in turn can lead to hypothermia and death. Sea kayakers are more likely to capsize after becoming exhausted, so it behoves them to practise several alternative methods of rescue, with more emphasis on remaining seated in the kayak if at all possible.

This book presents many alternatives, and recreational paddlers would profit by learning as many as they can. The tendency to panic in an emergency is reduced if the paddler practises under safe conditions, always with capable help nearby. Being prepared is the best insurance for surviving an emergency, and the peace of mind it can provide makes paddling more enjoyable.

Good instruction helps ease the anxiety of capsizing, and Derek Hutchinson is an excellent instructor. He has the ability to laugh at himself and see the humour in situations in which canoeists and kayakers sometimes find themselves. Those of us who learned rolling and rescue methods largely through trial and error could have profited from a book such as this. Let us hope that you never have to use these techniques in an emergency. But they are fun to practise, and good insurance.

JOHN D. HEATH
MAY 1992

Foreword to the Third Edition

Derek Hutchinson is fast becoming a canoe legend. In whatever guise you meet him – as an expedition leader, coach, writer, kayak designer or raconteur – the Hutchinson experience is never forgotten. Mention his name in kayaking circles and a smile passes the lips of all present. But, if you can't meet him in the flesh, then this book is the next best thing.

But what is this obsession with Eskimo rolling? I know he has a deep interest in Eskimo culture, but I had assumed that his experience at a coaching conference some years ago would have cured him of rolling for life. Derek had been asked to give a rolling demonstration and clinic at the conference and he had assumed it would be for relative beginnners. However, on entering the pool he found the poolside lined with many of the country's foremost kayak coaches jeering loudly for the first demonstration. Few had even bothered to change. This was the first time I had seen Derek visibly taken aback. After a slightly faltering entry into the kayak, he settled down into his characteristic patter only to be interrupted with shouts calling for a roll. White knuckles grasped the paddle shaft as Derek set up for the roll, then after a pause while a silent prayer was offered to the God of Succesful Rolling he took the plunge. The paddle thrashed violently and then a spluttering figure 'rolled up', fully realising why so few of the canoeists hadn't bothered changing – the pool was unheated.

The previous editions of this book have been referred to as the 'Rolling Bible'. I am sure a new generation of paddlers will also enjoy reading the words of the old master in this new, third edition.

GRAHAM LYON
CHAIR OF COACHING, BRITISH CANOE UNION
APRIL 1999

Acknowledgements

I consider John Heath to be one of the most knowledgeable men in the world on the subject of the native Eskimo Roll and I am especially grateful to him for his support and advice. The delightful extract from his writings is reproduced by John's kind permission and that of *Sea Kayaker* magazine. (The article was originally published in *Sea Kayaker*, Winter 1986, under the title 'Alaskan Eskimo Rolls'.)

Thanks are due to Paul Caffyn who kindly allowed me to reproduce extracts from his book *Obscured by Waves* (John McIndoe Ltd, New Zealand, 1979). I wish to make acknowledgement to the estate of F. Spencer Chapman and to Chatto & Windus for permission to include extracts from *Watkins' Last Expedition* by F. Spencer Chapman. My thanks to Reg and Molly Jones, the parents of the late Dr Mike Jones, for permission to use extracts from their son's wonderful book *Canoeing Down Everest* (Hodder & Stoughton, 1979). The extracts from *Eskimo Life* are by Fridof Nansen (Longman Green & Co., 1893).

A special thank you to Eric and Carolyn Powell for sharing with me the video which included the Greenland Trick Roll. Also to Keith Wickham of Silverscreen for his interest and encouragement, and to Robert Eaglestaff for the use of his photographs on the cover of the First Edition. Thank you as well to Graham Lyon for his Foreword to the Third Edition.

Special thanks must go to my wife Hélène for her help and support, and also for the time she spent correcting the text and so protecting the reader from my abysmal abuse of the English language.

Finally, this book was fun to write, and on looking back, I can say that was due mainly to the large number of people who contributed, either indirectly by their influence, or directly by baring their souls and relating their own personal rolling (or failing-to-roll) stories for your entertainment. If I named everyone here who helped or contributed, this page would look like a *Who's Who* of kayaking. Suffice it to say that many of them are well-known in Britain and the United States. I thank them for their honesty, time and willingness to share their sometimes embarrassing and frequently frightening experiences with the reader.

Introduction

The Eskimo Roll is a generic term given to the several techniques whereby the paddler of a kayak can, in the event of a capsize, right himself by the adroit use of the paddle, without ever having to leave the cockpit.

The Eskimo Roll is unique to the kayak. No other craft can be capsized and righted at will, without the user leaving the boat. The kayak is the most basic of all solo craft. It has neither sail nor engine, and the forward-facing paddler does not have even the advantage of a fulcrum which is afforded those who row. The kayak is propelled by a free-moving paddle held in both hands. To become proficient in a kayak it is necessary to master a number of strokes and manoeuvres. Of all these, the Eskimo Roll is probably the most absorbing to study and practise. Even for those who may never need to roll in a life threatening situation, learning the art will improve their technique and skill to such an extent that an accidental capsize will be a thing of the past. (I do not consider capsizes in large surf, on heavy rivers or while playing polo as accidental. In those contexts a capsize is merely part of that particular branch of the sport and is to be expected.)

This art of rolling was developed to a high degree by the Inuit kayak hunters of the Arctic, for whom it was a means of survival should they capsize while hunting in their kayaks for sea mammals or while fishing.

Very little has been written about the rolls used by the Alaskan Inuit. The rolls of the Greenlanders however, have been well documented by explorers and ethnographers, and it is upon these Greenland rolls that most of our modern recreational methods are based.

It was in 1927 that an Austrian named Edi Pawlata became the first European to perform an Eskimo Roll successfully. He was able to do this after studying the writings of Nansen and Jophansen. In 1930, whilst on a surveying expedition for a proposed Arctic air route, the English explorer, Gino Watkins, learned some of the Greenland methods of rolling.

I hadn't been canoeing long before I, too, desperately wanted to roll – well everyone else could, at least anybody who WAS anybody in the kayaking world.

My closest paddling friend at that time could roll, and because of this he had my undying admiration. Unfortunately, he seemed to spend an inordinately long time upside-down before finally regaining the surface. I would gaze horrified at his upturned hull, watching as his hands groped about to take up and experiment with different positions on the paddle. It was obvious to anyone that he had to work out each separate movement from scratch every time he capsized. I was amazed at his lung power, but not inspired to imitate his particular system. I wanted to spend as little time as possible underwater. After all, the Eskimos who had started this rolling business could not afford to spend any longer than necessary immersed in cold water. As things were, all I wanted to do when I capsized was get out of the boat as quickly and as effortlessly as possible and see the sky again. Something definitely had to be done about that.

I decided to explore the possibilities of learning to roll in a swimming pool. The nearest one, where the local slalom and white-water paddlers practised and played, was some miles away. Once there, it was easy to borrow one of the club's retired river boats and persuade the instructor in charge to teach me to roll. It was then I discovered that I was afflicted with a number of phobias which would inhibit the learning process:

1 Although I could hold my breath for quite a long time when I was standing in fresh air, I found that I was starved of oxygen after only a few seconds when hanging upside-down in a kayak. The smaller the cockpit, the quicker I seemed to run short of breath.

2 I hated getting water up my nose.

3 I was suddenly bereft of memory or reason the minute I went upside-down. Everything I learned the right way up fell out of my head when I was inverted.

I really did try very hard to please – and to roll – but I was obviously making mistakes which the instructor was unable to pinpoint. Because of this the faults remained uncorrected. I got more and more discouraged. Finally I gave up going to the pool.

But I still longed to be able to roll and because of this I hit upon a plan.

At that time, the cockpit of the kayak I used on the sea was so large that my knees had no support. In the event of a capsize I always fell out of the boat. It was important therefore that I made the seating position much more secure. To do this, I hacked off the front of the existing cockpit coaming. Then I rebuilt the whole affair on a smaller scale using sheet aluminium and large quantities of glass fibre. It did not look neat – in fact it looked downright ugly. From the side it looked as if the new coaming had taken a step upwards. More by luck than anything else it worked. Now I had something against which to brace my knees. It was a good start.

At that time I wore what is known as a two-stage life-jacket. That is, it had a block of flotation foam built into the inside of the inflatable bag. Thus the garment gave support even when it was deflated. I discovered that by fully inflating the bag and then capsizing, I was supported on the surface while still sitting in the kayak. My head was almost submerged, but by twisting sideways I could keep my mouth clear of the water and breathe. I also discovered that by putting the paddle out from me at right angles to the kayak, I could pull myself upright with a Support Stroke.

Every time I had one of these practice sessions I would release a little more air out of the life-jacket. This naturally caused me to sink even further. I took to wearing a nose-clip because when I was on my side, my head was underwater. I also had to make a conscious effort now to reach up towards the surface in order to get into the position to use the paddle.

As I was no longer using the controlled conditions of the swimming pool, I had to wait for calm days and use the sea near my home. The sea on the north-east coast is rarely flat for long, so these practice sessions were spread over many weeks. Each time I would release a little more air and each time I would sink a little further down. Eventually the time came when I was hanging almost perpendicular in the water. The inherent buoyancy of the life-jacket would allow me to sink no further.

The big day arrived. The water was calm and I decided to see if I could get into the same position, but this time I would capsize on the OPPOSITE side. I adjusted my nose-clip for the tenth time – then over I went. Sure enough I hung almost vertical, but this time I was on the WRONG side. By twisting my body from one side of the deck to the other, the buoyancy in the life-jacket took me round to my GOOD side. I opened my eyes and peered at the hazy light above me. I reached up and clutched the paddle in the now-familiar position. I pulled down on the extended blade and came to the surface. I had gone down on one side and up on the other. I could roll.

Knowing how to roll does not mean that you are obliged to do it all over the place, but it undoubtedly saves the time and difficulty that would normally be taken up by long, exhausting swims or traumatic deep-water rescues. It also means that only one half of the body gets wet, and an added bonus is that you will become a member of the (unofficial) Eskimo Roll Yarns Club.

It seems to be the case that just about everybody who can roll has a story to tell. These accounts range from the hilarious to the horrific. To show you how things can go wrong, even when the paddle is in the most steady and experienced of hands, I have included some lamp-swinging tales from the widely-paddled and famous. Some of these were gleaned through personal interview, and some from long-distance telephone conversations. In other cases I have been fortunate enough to have been granted permission to include extracts from the writings of well-known paddlers. By enjoying these accounts, you will see that a high level of skill means only that the conditions which capsize can still be harrowing if the water is rough, and quite humiliating if the water is calm. You will also come to realise that novices do not corner the market on fear.

This book is directed to all those kayak paddlers who wish to raise their level of skill or who wish to teach the art of rolling to others.

Derek C. Hutchinson

Author's note   Some illustrations are shown as having a 'fish-eye view'. In the instances where these are written upside-down, the book should be inverted to obtain this view. Throughout this book individuals are referred to as 'he'. This should, of course, be taken to mean 'he' or 'she' where appropriate.

CHAPTER I *Learning to roll*

There is no mystique about learning to Eskimo Roll, it is simply a matter of making the right movement at the right time. The reader may think this an oversimplification: after all, when hanging upside-down, waterlogged and disorientated, you are hardly in the best position to utilise what may seem complicated instructions.

This is true; nevertheless, a roll is not difficult to do – it is only difficult to learn, and anyone with perseverance and patience should be able to roll. Nor is physical strength really necessary, once the skill has been mastered.

When I started kayaking, in the early 1960s, anyone who was able to roll could be sure of collecting a small crowd of admiring onlookers. This was hardly surprising, as most of the instructors at that time taught the roll by performing a few expert and mind-boggling feats, after which the bewildered student would be sent off to practise. There was no structured method of teaching and mistakes usually went unnoticed or uncorrected. People soon got discouraged and the failure rate was high.

Since then, methods of teaching the roll have been made much more acceptable to beginners. Young children can be taught to hand roll without a paddle in less than fifteen minutes. Fears and misgivings can be overcome by practising simple confidence exercises. Those who have physical problems or who are physically handicapped, such as paraplegics or double amputees, can be taught to roll. Even those people who have only one useful arm, can be taught to paddle and roll.

Learning difficulties

The three main factors which inhibit the learning of the roll are: (1) psychological; (2) physical; (3) intellectual.

1 The student is assailed by uncontrolled anxiety and lack of confidence. Due to this troubled state of mind, instructions cannot be absorbed and his awareness of what is going on is only temporary. Because of fear and a haste born of desperation, the crucial movements are not done methodically and are badly timed.

2 The build of the student may give rise to difficulties when gripping with the thighs in order to stay seated in the inverted boat. Because of lack of co-ordination and timing, strength may be applied at the wrong time during the rolling sequence. Problems can also occur when there is a great difference in the ratio of arm strength to the weight of the torso.

3 The more analytical the student, often the more difficult he is to teach. During the teaching of the roll the student may be given a drill, i.e. a number of fixed movements which must be executed in sequence in a pre-determined manner. Failure often occurs when a student tries to analyse the movements he is making, such as relating a surface drill to an upside-down position. This makes him confused and prevents the spontaneity of the movement.

In the following pages I shall be dealing with 18 different Eskimo Rolls, together with a few of what can be called 'stunt' rolls.

The most important roll for any kayak paddler, whether on a river or the sea, is known as the Screw Roll. With this method, the hands are never moved from the normal paddling position. In this way there need be no interruption in the forward paddling stroke. When the roll is done on the move, the paddle appears to 'screw' the kayak forwards through the water – hence the name.

However, the roll I and most instructors prefer to teach first is known as the Pawlata Roll. It is done with the paddle held in an extended position, giving a longer leverage than is employed during the Screw Roll. Most novices find the Pawlata Roll the easiest to learn. The success rate is high and the movements employed lead directly into the teaching of the Screw Roll.

I am a right-handed person, but when I roll, my observant friends tell me that I roll left-handed, i.e. the surface position adopted with the paddle (or wind-up as it is called) immediately prior to starting the roll is done on my right-hand side. Thus I come to the surface on the left side.

Throughout the book, whenever reference is made to the 'driving' face of the paddle (also known as the 'wet' face or 'pressure' face) this is taken to mean the blade face which exerts pressure against the water during the forward paddling stroke. With spoon blades, the 'driving face' would refer to the inside of the convex curve.

The surface on the opposite side of the driving face is known as the back of the blade (sometimes referred to as the 'dry' face).

All the illustrations depicted in the book show the driving face of the paddle blade with a small crescent to represent the inside of the curve. The back of the blade is depicted as having a spine shown near the base of the blade.

All paddles are shown feathered for a right-handed person.

The first narrative I've chosen to include recalls one of my own personal and rather dramatic experiences of being rescued at sea.

My own attempt to lead a group of five other men on an unescorted crossing of the North Sea almost ended in tragedy. After 34 hours of paddling without sleep, punctuated by bouts of sickness, vomiting and hallucinations, we were finally forced to seek the assistance of a passing vessel.

When the offer came down from the bridge that they would be glad to take us on board, no one seemed reluctant to accept. The huge hull of the vessel protected us from the strong wind, so the waves were no longer breaking at the top. However, one moment the swell would take us high up the side, with its row upon row of black rivets, then we would drop down into the trough again. Getting us on board was going to be tricky.

Halfway along the side of the boat, there was a large steel door. It was about eight feet or so from the surface of the sea. As the swell rose up the ship's side, it reached its maximum height about three feet below the door. After a few minutes, the door opened and three very large crew members appeared. The method of leaving the water would be simple. One at a time, we would position ourselves as near to the black wall of rivets as possible. We would take the spray-covers off, hold the kayak's tow line in one hand and then, as the kayak rose on the swell almost to the waiting men, we would quickly hitch our behinds out of the cockpit and sit on the coaming with one arm extended up towards them. These stalwart men would then grab our hands and hoist us clear of our boats, while we still stayed in contact with our kayaks via the tow line. The boats would then be hauled aboard by the helpers. Like many ideas it was almost foolproof.

I was surprised how easily it all seemed to be going. One by one, I saw the others rise up towards the waiting men and, one by one, they hung for a few seconds, legs swinging in the fresh air, before being hoisted safely aboard. Gordon had a nasty moment. He put his hand up before becoming completely free from his cockpit. As the two strong crewmen clutched his arm, he discovered he was firmly stuck in the cockpit hole. As he and his boat went skywards together, there were hysterical cries of 'Whoa! Hold it! Down again!'

While this little drama was being enacted, I took time to remove the neoprene helmet I'd put on earlier, when things had been getting rough. I unzipped my buoyancy aid and I also loosened my anorak which had a zip down the front. The steam rose from my armpits and the interior of my clothing. I had already loosened my tow line in readiness for the big lift, but somehow the thing had got itself tangled underneath something on the rear deck. I twisted round as far as I could and leaned backwards and to the side, stretching out my hand as I did so to untangle the line.

At the moment of jerking it free I over-balanced, almost against the side of the ship. The freezing North Sea felt as if it was invading and paralysing every steaming part of my body. I went upside-down and it was as if someone had tightened an ice clamp on my head. I opened my eyes and peered through the brown murk and the bubbles. There was no sound of wind now. No sound of voices – just a rushing in my ears. What the hell was that? I realised the buoyancy aid had floated up over my arms and it was now around my head. I peered past the red haze that seemed to hang next to my eyes. Thankfully, I could make out the yellow of my paddle, still floating next to me on the surface where I'd put it while I'd been loosening my clothing. I grabbed at it, took it into my hand and felt for the ovalling that would give me the correct angle for the roll. I couldn't take the chance of a Screw Roll not working, so I moved my right hand quickly along the shaft until I could feel the start of the blade – I wasn't taking any chances on this one.

As I struck out with the paddle I was aware of the massive blackness of the ship's hull next to me. I yanked down with my outstretched arm and I felt the kayak coming round with me with the ease of a lump of lead. As I broke the surface, water gushed out of my nose, clothes, ears and mouth. The water didn't drain out of my sleeves. They just hung like two sausage balloons. Never mind! I was up and even the grey sky looked good. Perhaps tomorrow was going to be a better day . . .

Graham Lyons demonstrating a Screw Roll during a fun session at a National Coaching Conference, Nottingham. Photo: Derek C. Hutchinson

CHAPTER 2 *Where to learn*

The learning of a skill like the Eskimo Roll is made comfortable and more enjoyable if it can be done in a warm swimming pool, with clear chlorinated water (not that chlorinated water ever did me much good!) and a knowledgeable instructor standing close at hand.

I would recommend these conditions but realise that many people have no access to either instructor or pool. Because of this, I have tried to cater for the student who has no professional help and has to use whatever water is at hand.

If possible, try to enlist the assistance of a well-informed friend, perhaps a fellow paddler who has read this book or who at least can act sensibly under your instructions. So, when in the text I refer to the instructor, please read that as also being your 'well-informed friend'. It is impossible to overestimate the safety value of having another person – whoever it is – present nearby during practice sessions.

Assuming that you are unable to practise at a swimming pool, choose a quiet lake or tide pool, a sheltered bay or a stretch of placid river. The shore or sides should shelve gently so that during certain stages of practice, the paddle can be supported on a firm surface. There should be no swell or breaking waves in the training area. A spot which is about four to five feet deep is ideal.

Dress comfortably for the weather conditions and water temperature. This may mean a wet-suit of some kind. If the water is very cold, a neoprene helmet would be an advantage.

Winter, 1967, and as gale force winds blow across the cold North Sea, the author practises rolls in his first successful kayak design. The large painting of an Eskimo, which decorated the fore-deck, can just be seen vanishing under the water. PHOTO COURTESY DEREK C. HUTCHINSON

I don't mind repeating the warning that beginners should never practise in dangerous waters. They should remember that even experienced kayakers are not immune from trouble. **Reg Lake**, *who is a skilled kayak surfer and who has a number of white-water descents to his credit, recalls a desperate occasion in San Francisco Bay.*

I called my friend but he wasn't home, so, as I thought he might already be on the water, I headed down to Fort Point near the South Tower of the Golden Gate Bridge. I'd had my weather radio on and it told me that swells of 13 feet every 14 seconds could be expected. He wasn't there so I paddled out alone.

The waves were so big they seemed to move in slow motion. There was a surfer out there who was also a kayaker. We agreed to act as back-up for each other. Looking back, I suppose we didn't really have any back-up.

I remember one huge set that came in. I had to paddle out fast at an angle to it, in order to escape it. It closed out and I got hit. I did a roll, hung in there, and worked my way along the break and came out of it. My spray-skirt had blown and I'd taken water into the boat. I paddled out again to get set up in line with the waves. Then I saw a huge set coming square in beneath the bridge. I was much further inshore than I wanted to be.

I started paddling out fast at an angle to it so as to minimise its effect on me. As I'm paddling out, this horrifying wave is coming in towards me. A 13-foot wave looks more like a 20-footer when you're out there! I started to rise up the face of this thing, when it started to break. I began to free-fall. It all seemed to happen slowly. Then the boat hit the green water at the bottom of the wave and I got whipped over on the left side. I would normally go for a Screw Roll but I was upside-down and flattened on to the rear deck. It raised my butt off the seat and I could feel the boat being stripped off me. I knew the importance of staying attached to the kayak but I couldn't hold it. I ended up trying to hook it with my feet but it was no good.

By the time I surfaced, the boat was 20 feet away. I went to swim for it but another wave came in and took it further away. I tried to get to it one more time, this time swimming with the paddle. It seemed as if it was still moving further away and I knew I wasn't going to catch it up.

The sea seemed pretty slack at this point so I decided to see if I could land on the sandy beach round the point just outside the Gate. I shouted and told the surfer what I intended to do but he just shrugged and yelled 'Yeah!' The only other alternative was to go in with the waves but these were breaking against the wall and exploding about 30 feet into the air. I kept on swimming, using the paddle. This was to be a good decision, but I didn't know this at the time. I thought about sharks and then I thought, 'There are more important things to think about . . . Back to the business in hand!' I kept working my way further and further around the point. Every 14 seconds, a wave would come through. I'd go under then come up out of it, clear my nose and keep going. I got round the outside, working my way closer and closer to the beach.

I thought I would body-surf in but the waves would catch me and just tumble me like a rag doll. As I got closer in, I tried to conserve energy but another wave would come and I'd be underwater with no light and no air for long periods of time. When I finally surfaced, I'd be rushing back out again, away from the beach. With what little breath I had, I'd go for the next wave and half body-surf, half tumble in towards the beach but it would seem a long time before I would be able to surface. Then I would be rushing backwards again away from the beach. Twice I could feel my feet and ankles touch the bottom but there was no way of getting a grip and stopping myself going out again. I was desperately short of breath, but I decided to try to put some air inside the dry-suit top I was wearing. In this way, I thought, I would float higher in the water.

As I was blowing it up I noticed a kind of wheezing. It frightened me because it seemed to me that I had water on my lungs. The thought came to me suddenly: 'This is what drowning is like and nobody has ever lived to tell about it!' The thought scared the hell out of me. At that point, I turned and went back out through the breakers, where there was less turbulence and where I could put a breath more air into the dry-top and get my breath back.

I was in good physical shape and I was wearing neoprene shorts and the dry-suit top. But I also knew that I was losing body heat and that my situation was deteriorating fast. I had the uneasy feeling that time was of the essence. As I struggled to get back out through the surf, I saw the Coast Guard boat going out through the Gate. I set the paddle straight up in the air and waved it but the boat kept on going. I got an awful sinking feeling, but I thought that perhaps it was on a more important mission – although my position seemed pretty important to me! As it happened, the boat went straight out and then came around outside the breakers and started to make its way back in towards me. At the same time I kept on swimming out. Eventually it came alongside and I was taken aboard.

I felt relieved, but also embarrassed. You see I felt I was representing the sport and I was disappointed in myself for breaking one of my own rules about going out with a minimum of three. I had given a lot of thought to normal precautions: I was dressed properly; I'd got a weather forecast; I had a life-jacket and I was carrying flares. I had no expectation of ever coming out of the boat and knew the importance of staying in it. I thought that I would stay in it and roll up no matter what – but as things turned out, I didn't have that choice.

Chapter 3 *Equipment*

The kayak

It is important to feel at home and snug in the cockpit of the kayak you intend to roll. A moulded bucket seat will cradle the behind firmly and prevent any tendency to slip sideways. By pressing the feet down firmly on to a footrest, it should be possible to force the thighs outwards and knees upwards into a locked position under the cockpit coaming. If the seat is badly fitting or too wide, it can be made to fit tighter by means of soft foam or neoprene pads glued to the sides. Large, long cockpits can be made suitable for rolling by fitting wooden knee bars. A temporary brace for the thighs can be formed by laying a piece of wood across the lap and jamming it at the sides under the coaming.

Most kayaks of about two feet wide or less are easy to roll. Those with a pronounced sheer, coupled with ample buoyancy at the bow and stern, giving the kayak a banana-like profile, are the easiest. The cockpits of all modern white-water river kayaks have knee and thigh braces incorporated into their design.

The spray-cover/skirt

The purpose of a spray-cover is to prevent water from entering the cockpit area. The tighter the cover fits the more likely it is to be watertight. A release strap should be securely fitted to the front or side, enabling the cover to be removed quickly and without damage in the event of an emergency exit. Take care that the spray-cover is not worn inside out. This could put the release strap out of reach or cause too much strain on the stitching and thus cause the strap to break.

Paddles

If possible use a paddle with which you are familiar. Novices can have difficulty with highly specialised spoon blades unless they are familiar with them. I personally use a straight-bladed sea paddle – it is uncomplicated and when I roll it doesn't 'flutter' or do strange things in the water.

INSTRUCTOR'S NOTE An instructor will find it much easier to notice faults in paddle presentation, if the students have the driving face of their paddle blades painted a different colour from that of the back of the blade.

Comfort items

With practice it will soon be possible to open the eyes when submerged. In the early stages, however, a nose-clip and a pair of swimming goggles or a diver's face mask can be used to help give the learner a clear underwater view of the surface and the whereabouts of the paddle. Some people may frown on using such aids, but if they help to master the Eskimo Roll, then, in my view, they are well worthwhile.

Find a quiet corner of a swimming pool and learn to breathe out slowly through the nose underwater. If you learn to breathe out slowly like this when rolling, it will prevent water forcing its way into your sinuses and you will avoid the discomfort that this causes.

Not only is it important to learn to open the eyes underwater, but also to keep them open and alert when on top of the water! **Ron Miller** *(who is one of the British Canoe Union's senior coaches) tells the following story to illustrate this fact.*

It was a cold overcast day in 1966. The sea was the colour of cold steel. A Very Important Person, the National Coach of the British Canoe Union, was about to examine the first group of paddlers silly enough to present themselves for the Advanced Sea Kayak award. One now well-known author-kayaker – but at that time just an ordinary Derek Hutchinson – decided to have cold (feet?) and withdrew from the group. He joined the aforementioned VIP who also showed little enthusiasm for joining the candidates, as they launched their kayaks from the beach near the Haugh Battery at Hartlepool.

All of the candidates were using Eskimo kayaks, mostly home-built lathe and canvas versions of the Tyne 'Eskimo' design. Let me hasten to assure you that the only reason for using this relatively unstable kayak, with its very limited carrying capacity was that, after many years of dedicated aversion to getting wet, other than surfing or showering, we would have to perform a 'first-time ten-second roll' and none of us could roll very well. However, using the BCU approved-type life-jacket, all one really needed to do after capsizing was to wait until the life-jacket floated you to the surface and then perform a good Support Stroke. For those of you so young as to imagine that the main purpose of an Eskimo Roll is to return you to the upright position as soon as reasonably possible, allow me to explain that a 'first-time ten-second roll' was nothing so realistic! It was, instead, a masochistic exercise, demonstrating the victim's determination to remain inverted, cold and uncomfortable whilst counting, '1001, 1002, 1003 . . .' until, at '1011', you were permitted to rejoin the human race in their regular habit of imbibing oxygen cocktail.

We were instructed to launch, paddle out to sea and demonstrate the usual strokes and turns, finishing with the ten-second roll. This was to be followed by a capsize and swim ashore.

I launched as instructed, and moved out from the beach, played around for a while then looked for the least inconvenient point from which to swim ashore. This seemed to be the North Pier. I would have calm water and a little help from the current. That was a bad decision! I had not noticed the solitary person sitting on the edge of the pier. I certainly did not see the almost transparent line which stretched from this person to the sea! My first realisation of its existence was when it made contact at a point about mid-way between the top of my life-jacket and my chin. The ten-second roll had started. When you are upside-down with a fishing line across your windpipe you completely forget about '1001, 1002 . . . etc.' Instead, your concentration is focused on such things as, 'How the hell do you get out of this?' and 'How the hell do you shout for help when your head's underwater?' The first attempt to roll was ineffective because the paddle had gone over the line and it was impossible to move it without tightening the line on the throat! They say that in a situation such as this, your past life passes through your mind. I didn't find this. I was too busy being frightened – and hating fishermen.

At this point fate took a hand. The movement of the water must have generated some slack in the line and my BCU-approved life-jacket decided to bring me to the surface furthest from the fisherman. I can only guess at what happened next, but I believe that as I had capsized towards the fisherman I had wound some line down with me and then taken more line when I had attempted to roll.

Once I let go of the paddle to change grip, to roll on the other side, my wrist became free and this gave even more slack line which I was able to free from my neck. I then completed the roll on the side away from the pier.

It seemed to me that I had been under for at least half an hour but in fact it must have been little more than the prescribed 10 seconds. I know this because the VIP, who was too far away to have seen the line, shouted to me through his hand-held amplifier, 'You do not seem very stable in your canoe, Ron. You must make up your mind which side you're going to roll on. You tried to come up on the same side as you capsized.'

Chapter 4 *Confidence exercises*

The student should feel relaxed and at home in the kayak, whether sitting upright or hanging upside-down in the water. The best way to achieve this is by working through a few carefully graded confidence exercises which eventually lead to the complete roll.

One of the novice's greatest fears is that of being trapped upside-down and unable to leave the cockpit. It is a natural fear, but with a little experience it will soon be realised that one of the most difficult parts of the operation is to stay firmly fixed in the boat.

It is possible to paddle for many years on sheltered waters and never experience a capsize and bail-out. While learning to roll, however, a capsize will be a deliberate part of the process and a capsize and bail-out is not an unusual occurrence. In anticipation of this, what is called the Capsize Drill should be practised. This will give experience of the ease with which the spray-cover can be removed and of the actual difficulty of remaining stuck in the cockpit.

If possible the first capsize should not be done alone. A nose-clip may be worn to minimise discomfort, but it is worth remembering that accidental capsizes give little time for preparation. Be brave, and when upside-down breathe out through the nose.

Capsize drill

1 Before the capsize, hold the paddle in the normal paddling position and then capsize.

2 Wait until the boat is completely upside-down and has come to rest.

3 Keep holding on to the paddle with one hand. Then with the other hand (preferably with your eyes open) locate the release strap and pull it firmly but carefully to remove the spray-cover.

4 Lean forwards. Place both hands on the cockpit coaming just behind the hips, then push the cockpit forwards and away. (Yes, I know you still have hold of the paddle in one hand – awkward, isn't it?)

During this manoeuvre the legs should be kept almost straight.

I tell students to remove themselves from the kayak in the same way as they take off their trousers. I know of no one who leans backwards to do this.

INSTRUCTOR'S NOTE

To give confidence, the first capsize may be done without the spray-cover in place. If this is the case the student should bang three times on the upturned hull before getting out. This will be an indication that all is well and that the student is in full control.

Beware of a hasty exit made by twisting the body backwards along the rear deck. If this happens the whole exercise must be done again.

If on open water, once on the surface do not be tempted to turn the kayak upright again. The air trapped inside the upturned hull will help to keep the boat afloat. Take hold of one of the end loops or toggles, then still holding on to the paddle, get the boat to shore using a backstroke leg kick.

Never grasp hold of a capsized kayak in the centre, as this might cause it to turn over. If this happens and the boat has no bulkheads or inadequate buoyancy, it could fill up with water and sink, or at best, make swimming to shore very difficult.

In this watercolour of 1893, the kayak hunters are depicted running before a following sea, i.e. wind and waves are approaching from the rear. The man on the left appears to be steering by means of a low brace, while the centre paddler is supporting himself on the wave with a high brace. The cautious hunter on the right is holding his paddle in an extended position. In this way he is ready to apply either a high or a low brace. FROM NANSEN, *Eskimo Life*

CHAPTER 5 *The Hip Flick*
Hip rotation or hip mobility

Given some fragmentary instruction and plenty of luck, it is possible to force an inverted kayak back to the surface again after a capsize by what can only be described as brute force and ignorance.

To convert this thrashing, awkward and clumsy manoeuvre into the enviably smooth, efficient sweep which swiftly restores the craft to its upright position, one must master a simple body movement known as the 'Hip Flick'.

The following exercises will introduce the reader to the Hip Flick and thus incorporate it into the rolling sequence.

In these exercises, when use of a support is mentioned, this will be either the rail or gutter round the outside edge of a pool or a helper's paddle held firmly on the surface of the water. On open water, a paddle can be used in the same way – if your partner has a good wet-suit – or you can use the loop or toggle at the bow of the partner's kayak.

Exercises

Exercise 1

Fig. 5.1
Wobbling the kayak from side to side

1 With and without support, and with knees pressed firmly against the underside of the deck, practise wobbling the kayak from side to side (*see* fig. 5.1). This will increase hip mobility as you learn to keep the upper body steady, using only the hips to move the kayak.

Exercise 2

Fig. 5.2
Place both your hands
on your support

Fig. 5.3
Gradually increase the
rotation

Fig. 5.4
When the kayak is almost
out of the water your body
should still be horizontal

2 Place both hands on your support, with knuckles upwards (*see* fig. 5.2). Using the hip movement just described, practise tipping the kayak further and further on the supported side. Gradually increase the rotation (*see* fig. 5.3), taking your head and body deeper and deeper into the water until you can bring yourself up from the completely inverted position. By this time you will, of course, be holding your support with only one hand. Once you feel confident using your hand, and then just the fingers of one hand for support, a good way to practise is to have your head supported in the hands of your friend or instructor and Hip Flick to the surface (*see* fig. 5.5).

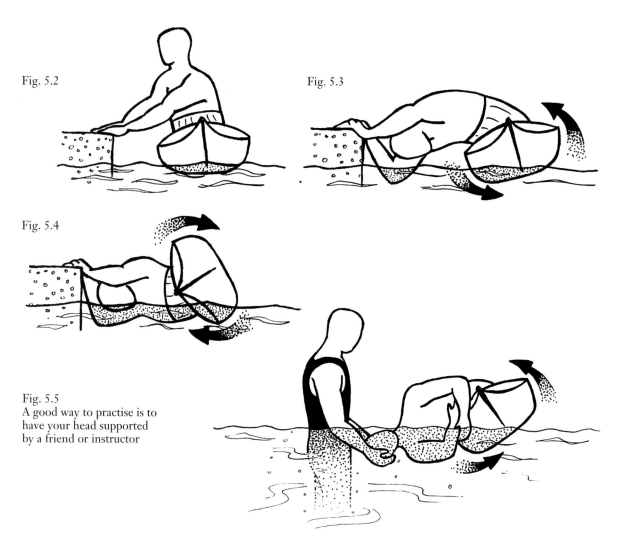

Fig. 5.2

Fig. 5.3

Fig. 5.4

Fig. 5.5
A good way to practise is to
have your head supported
by a friend or instructor

3 Now this next point may seem superfluous to my more spatially orientated reader. But, believe me, it does occasionally happen that the person trying to achieve complete inversion and still hanging grimly on to the support, finds it easier to swap hands halfway round. This means that, when inverted, they are now holding the support with what was their 'outer' hand when upright. Naturally this means that this hand is no help at all in regaining the upright position. It is as well for the observant instructor to spot this error before drowning occurs.

Most people find it helpful to keep the centre of gravity low by leaning forward. However, some people prefer to lean backwards, while others will find that whether they lean forwards or backwards is decided for them by the shape of their kayak.

For those whose choice it is to lean backwards, it must be emphasised that this only works satisfactorily if the head actually touches the rear deck and remains there till the kayak is righted. This is because, as has already been stated, it is important to keep the centre of gravity as low as possible.

Do not practise these exercises alone. Someone standing on the side of the pool or on the beach is better than no one at all.

Although I have stressed that it is essential to have someone standing by in case things go wrong, there is the odd occasion when a kayaker prefers to be left to his own devices. **Ray Calverley** *(four-time British Slalom Champion) remembers a particular Olympic Games' experience.*

In the 1972 Olympic Games, I unfortunately capsized in what is called the 'washing machine'. I went upside-down and travelled down the side of the big rock. I was nearly running out of air . . . but no way was I going to fall out in the Olympic Games for any reason. I was hanging on to the last of the air and eventually I got to the flat bit below the rock where I managed to roll up. Would you believe I then had to desperately beat two German soldiers about the head, who were busy trying to rescue me. You see I'd have been disqualified if they'd assisted me.

There's a tail-end to this story. The incident was reported in *Punch* magazine. There was a cartoon in which the wife – who was watching television – was saying to the husband, 'Come quickly, this is the British competitor in the Canoe Slalom . . .' The husband comes in but says, 'Well what's he doing upside-down then?'

CHAPTER 6 *Eskimo rescues*

Before embarking on the series of exercises that will gradually and painlessly lead the student ultimately to a successful Eskimo Roll, it is only fair to point out that in the process the occasional unsolicited capsize might occur.

If the water and the air are warm, as in a swimming pool, the experience can be quite refreshing. It is a different matter though, if the capsize takes place in the open air with a breeze blowing and the water cold. In this case it is not so much the capsize that is the nuisance, as having to get out of the boat, wade ashore and empty out. If the spray-cover is tight, then replacing it with cold hands also adds to the whole time-consuming business.

To save time or loss of continuity, and also to keep warm and comfortable, I recommend a method of rescue which a Greenland Eskimo might have used on a paddling companion who had failed to roll.

The rescue is known as the Eskimo Rescue and there are two kinds, depending upon the direction of approach made by the rescuer. They are (1) the Bow Rescue and (2) the Side Rescue.

(1) Bow Rescue

This is the most common method of Eskimo Rescue and of the two methods it is the easier to learn. It is probably the most useful when learning to roll, as the rescuer can position his boat a few feet away, pointing in the right direction to give immediate assistance.

Start by holding on to the toggle of the helper's kayak and let your boat go over until at least one ear is in the water. Then pull yourself up. Twist the kayak up first and lift your head out of the water last of all. Keep practising this until you are completely upside-down. As with the Hip Flick exercise you may find that your hand grip on the bow has to change before you become fully inverted. To do this, let go of the bow for a second, then renew your grip and pull yourself upright again. (*See* figs 6.1 and 6.2.)

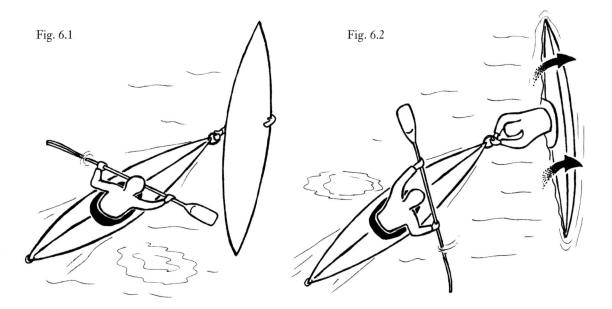

Fig. 6.1

Fig. 6.2

Bow Rescue

Fig. 6.1
Locate the rescuer's bow

Fig. 6.2
Grip the toggle and pull up

Practise this on both sides. Most people have a favourite side which, as in Eskimo Rolling, has nothing to do with being left- or right-handed.

Being able to accept an Eskimo Rescue will be helpful and especially time-saving when you are practising the various support strokes described in the next chapter. To take advantage of this kind of assistance, make sure your helper is only a few feet away and pointing towards you. If you fail while attempting one of the strokes and find yourself upside-down, here is what you do:

1 Release your grip on the paddle.

2 Lean forwards and bang both hands on your upturned hull. The sudden loud noise will let your rescuer know that you need assistance (*see* fig. 6.3).

3 Push your hands up into the fresh air and move them backwards and forwards in an arc above the surface (*see* fig. 6.4). Each sweep should cover about two to three feet. Doing this will give you a better chance of locating the rescuer's bow when it is presented to you. It will also save your rescuer unnecessary time and manoeuvring, and you will not have to wait so long. Once you feel the bow touch your hand, take a firm grip and pull to the surface.

**Practices for the
Bow Rescue**

Fig. 6.3
Bang on the
bottom of the hull

Fig. 6.4
Move the arms
back and forth

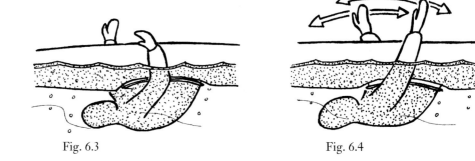

Fig. 6.3   Fig. 6.4

INSTRUCTOR'S
NOTE

As the capsized paddler begins to pull upright, the tendency will be for him to push the bow of the rescuing craft away from him, thus making his pull to the surface more difficult. To compensate for this, the rescuer should maintain position by paddling forwards, pushing the bow in towards his capsized partner.

(2) Side Rescue

In the normal paddling situation this is by far the most useful method. There is also less chance of a rescuer charging in at high speed and forcing the bow of his boat up the nose of the very person he is trying to help, who may just at that moment have decided to come up for air.

The following instructions are directed to the rescuer:

1 After being made aware of a capsize and the need for assistance (the noise of hand banging), paddle fast to a position parallel to the upturned kayak.

2 With one hand, grasp the wrist that is waving about between the two kayaks. This will stop you moving forwards (*see* fig. 6.5).

3 With your free hand, quickly place your paddle well across the upturned hull without releasing the grasped wrist.

4 Now place this grasped hand on your paddle shaft. The capsized paddler can then reach round and, by taking a two-handed grip on your paddle, will now be able to pull himself to the surface (*see* fig. 6.6).

It is vital that the person needing assistance WAITS UNTIL HIS CORRECT HAND IS PLACED ON TO THE PADDLE SHAFT by the rescuer, otherwise he may clutch it on the wrong side, i.e. farthest away from the rescuer. If this happens an hysterical little scene is then

Side Rescue

Fig. 6.5
The position of the
hands when inverted

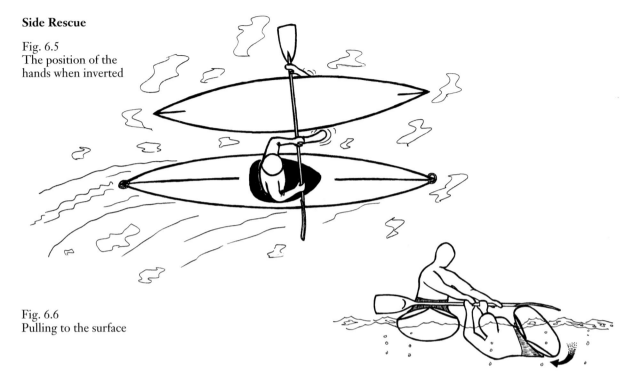

Fig. 6.6
Pulling to the surface

enacted as the underwater hero tries to pull himself on a paddle shaft, the weight of which is now effectively locking the kayak in the upside-down position.

Swimming with the kayak

In this simple exercise (*see* fig. 6.7) the paddler remains seated in the kayak, capsizes, and then, without getting out of the boat, swims to the side of the pool, or the alternative support used for the Hip Flick exercise. If you MUST practise this alone, make sure that you do so next to a shelving sandy bottom.

For the first try, position yourself about a yard from your support. Capsize towards it and begin your arm swim movement as soon as you touch the water. There is a good reason for this, because if you wait until you are completely upside-down before you begin to swim, you may find that disorientation causes you to swim *in the opposite direction*. Practice will dictate which swimming stroke suits you the best.

Swimming with the kayak

Fig. 6.7
Pull upright on the pool rail, or on a firmly held paddle shaft, or swim into shallow water

I prefer to swim doing a dog paddle with one arm and overarm with the other. Some lucky people find that they can even breathe during their swim but I am afraid that I am not one of them. Whatever method you choose, keep at it until you can cover about 20 feet.

Apart from being one of the accepted confidence-builders for the Eskimo Roll, this exercise also has other applications. It can help you retrieve a lost paddle or assist you in meeting your rescuer halfway during an Eskimo Rescue.

This record of an Eskimo Rescue in rough water is almost a hundred years old. The hunter has placed his paddle across his companion's kayak to assist with a side rescue. Meanwhile, an inflated seal skin, part of the stricken hunter's equipment, floats free. Nansen tells us: ' ... his first thought is for his comrade, to whose assistance he ... hastens. He runs his kayak alongside the other, lays his paddle across both, bends down so that he gets hold underwater of his companion's arm, and with a jerk drags him up upon his side, so that he too can get hold of the paddle and in an instant raise himself upon an even keel.' FROM NANSEN, *Eskimo Life*

CHAPTER 7

Extended Paddle Position and basic support strokes

It is worth mentioning at the outset that there are two basic paddle strokes (usually learned in the early stages of the sport) that will give an immediate advantage to hopeful students of the Eskimo Roll. These are (1) the Support Stroke, also known as the Brace; and (2) the Sculling for Support Stroke.

These two strokes are usually taught to beginners with the paddle held in the Extended Paddle Position, in order to obtain maximum leverage. It is especially important for the student to practise these support strokes using the Extended Paddle Position because this method of leverage is needed for several Eskimo Rolls.

Extended Paddle Position

Fig. 7.1
Basic grip

Fig. 7.2
Support position

Extended paddle position

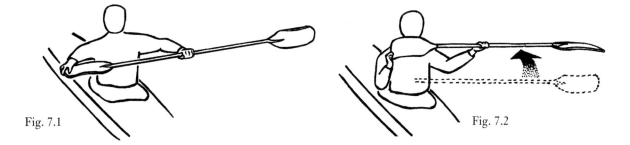

Fig. 7.1   Fig. 7.2

METHOD **1** Hold the paddle horizontally at arm's length (fig. 7.1). Cup one hand to hold the nearest corner of the horizontal blade, thumb on top. Move the other hand along the loom until the space between the hands is the same as when you are holding the paddle in the normal paddling position. The hand on the shaft should be held so that the knuckles are in line with the upper edge of the vertical blade.
2 Bring the paddle towards the chest through a 90° arc. Do not change the grip on either hand. Do not bend the wrists. Simply bend and drop the elbows. The arms should pivot at the elbows (*see* fig. 7.2).

25

If you have managed to follow this correctly, then:

Hip Flick practice in the pool

Figs. 7.3, 7.4, 7.5
The paddle can be held in the Extended Paddle Position or biased towards one end as shown

(a) the cupped hand will now be found to be supporting the *lower* edge of the held blade;
(b) the knuckles of the other hand will be facing backwards;
(c) the elbows will be pointing down towards the water;
(d) the extended blade is now parallel to the water – driving face down.

You are now holding your paddle in the Extended Paddle Position.

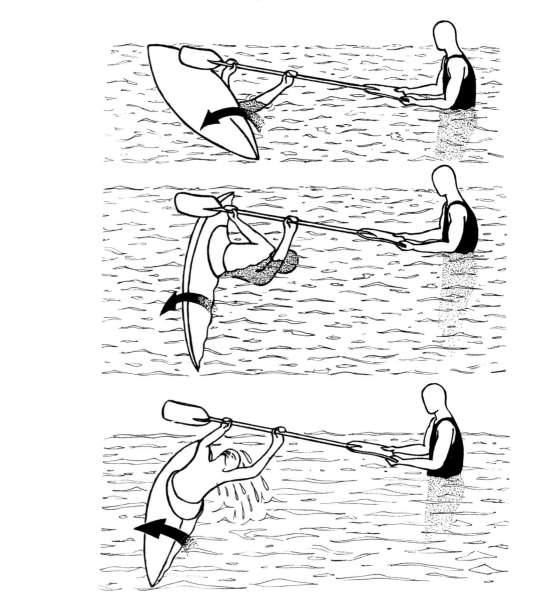

Fig. 7.3

Fig. 7.4

Fig. 7.5

EXERCISE   It is important to follow the sequence every time, to ensure the hands are always in the correct position. To get the 'feel' of the extended paddle blade in the support position, try the following exercise:

1 Hold your paddle in the Extended Paddle Position. The extended end of the paddle will need good support. This can be given by:

(a) being held in the hands of your partner, whether he is in a kayak or standing in the water (*see* figs 7.3, 7.4, 7.5);
(b) positioned on the river bank;
(c) on shelving sand, about two feet below the surface of the water;
(d) on your partner's deck (although the paddle might tend to slip about).

2 You now have a floating pivot (the kayak) and a secondary pivot, which is a point between your hands. As you pull down on the extended, supported end of the paddle and push up on the hand-held blade, the secondary pivot will help to right the body weight but the floating pivot (the kayak) should still be righted entirely by the movement of the hips.

3 Practise leaning over, taking the body deeper and deeper into the water and hanging your body weight from the paddle. Still maintaining your two-handed grip, practise the pull-down and Hip Flick, until you can right yourself and the kayak from the deepest possible position.

(1) Support Stroke or Brace

To get the feel of how the water will support you, try the following simple experiment:

1 Adopt the Extended Paddle Position and place the face of the extended blade on the surface of the water.

2 Pull down sharply on the shaft, at the same time compensating with upward pressure from the cupped hand.

3 As the extended blade presses into the water, if the speed of the movement is correct, the result will be audible and you will feel the support given by the water.

Practise this movement, leaning further and further over. You will feel that the downward pressure enables you to push back upright again.

METHOD   To put the stroke to the test, sit upright with the paddle in the Extended Paddle Position.

1   Hold the extended blade about an inch above the water. Now lean over until you are just off balance and about to capsize.

2   As you feel yourself about to go over, pull sharply down on to the water with the paddle as before. The capsize will be checked immediately and the kayak restored to its normal position.

3   Let me give a word of caution here. Before lifting the blade back out of the water, quickly twist it forwards through 90°, so that it slices out cleanly. If the paddle is underwater and you attempt to extract it while the blade is still parallel to the surface, the pressure you have been exerting in one direction to bring you to the surface, could cause you to capsize if exerted in the opposite direction.

At a beginner's level, the Support Stroke should be practised until at least one inch or so of the spray-cover can be dipped under the water. On a more advanced level, which is probably outside the scope of the reader/student, the paddle is held in the normal paddling position. Even with this shorter leverage, it is possible to achieve almost a half roll.

(2) Sculling for Support Stroke

Anything which travels across the surface of the water and is angled so that its leading edge is high, will stay on the surface until the forward movement ceases. This is true of, for example, a thrown flat stone, skim board or water ski. It is also the essential principle of the stroke known as Sculling for Support.

The author is sculling for support while testing modifications to his new Baidarka Explorer design in high winds and bitter winter conditions. The air temperature is below freezing, but the neoprene mitts have open palms to ensure a positive grip on the paddle shaft should a roll prove necessary.
Photo: Derek C. Hutchinson

Sculling for Support Stroke

Fig. 7.6
The stroke cycle

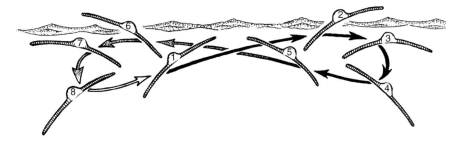

METHOD

When beginners are learning to scull for support it is often best to adopt the Extended Paddle Position.

1 The paddle is held in the Extended Paddle Position at an angle of 90° to the kayak and the blade is placed on the water.

2 It is then moved backwards and forwards in a small arc of about three feet.

3 During the movement the leading edge of the blade is kept tilted upwards so that it is always trying to climb towards the surface.
(*See* fig. 7.6.)

4 At the point where the blade changes direction, its trailing edge is raised to create a new leading edge. In this way the paddler planes or sculls back and forth just below the surface.

This sculling action will either give you support while leaning over or raise you in a controlled manner back to the upright position. Throughout the stroke the shaft of the paddle should be angled as acutely as possible with the surface of the water. The sculling action is controlled by a wrist flick movement of the extended hand.

THE STROKE CYCLE

Figure 7.6 gives a diagramatic representation of the paddle blade position during the Sculling for Support Stroke. You are looking down the paddle shaft towards the blade, on your right side. The left side of the diagram is therefore towards the front of your boat. Remember that the knuckles of the right hand will be in line with the top edge of the blade.

1 The angled blade is pulled rearwards and planes towards the surface.

2 This is the end of the upward plane. The leading edge is still high.

3 The blade is pulled downwards.

4 The direction is changed; the new blade angle means that the leading edge is now on the right side.

5 The blade is planed forwards.

6 Stop planing forwards when the blade reaches the point which is almost the limit of forward movement.

7 The blade is now pulled sharply downwards while at the same time adopting the angle in position 8.

8 From this position, repeat the stroke cycle.

Fig. 7.7
Practice for the controlling hand

Fig. 7.8
Paddle held in normal paddling position

To confirm in your mind which is the controlling hand during the Sculling for Support Stroke, try sculling with the shaft of the paddle held cradled in the crook of your elbow (*see* fig. 7.7). You will discover that the downward pressure will enable you to open the crooked elbow allowing you still to support the shaft, while you continue the stroke

Fig. 7.9
Paddle held in extended
paddling position

Fig. 7.10
The figure-of-eight move-
ment shortens as the lean
increases

with the lower, controlling hand. Once you feel confident with this
exercise, try sculling with the blade held in the normal paddling
position (*see* fig. 7.8).

INSTRUCTOR'S
NOTE

Knuckles which start off in line with the top edge of the paddle blade at
stage 1 of the stroke cycle must remain in the same position on the
paddle shaft throughout the stroke.

It will be seen that the paddle blade is always in a support position
even at the change of direction at the extremities of the arc.

As the paddler's lean increases, so the figure-of-eight will become
more flattened, making the stroke appear to be on almost the same
plane (*see* figs 7.9, 7.10).

The length of the arc of the sweep will also become much shorter to
perhaps only a foot long, thus compressing the whole stroke movement,
and making the figure-of-eight less definable.

There are some common faults which should be recognised and
corrected:

1 Instead of keeping the paddle at 90° to the kayak, the paddler has a tendency to twist round gradually and attempt to scull progressively towards the stern. This will cause a capsize.

2 Much splashing and frothing means the paddle is on top of the water instead of being JUST BENEATH the surface.

3 In the effort of concentration, the paddler forgets to change the angle of the blade and thus slices the paddle deeper and deeper.

At an advanced level the kayak may be allowed to lean over slowly until completely upside-down and then sculled up to the surface again. By leaning back during the sculling stroke until the head touches the rear deck, it is possible to hold the kayak in an almost completely capsized position and still keep your face out of the water. To recover from this position, press down sharply on the extended paddle, at the same time twisting the hips upwards and away from the supported side.

During this stroke, let the lower leg relax and straighten somewhat, while the upper leg is tensed and crooked firmly under the cockpit coaming.

Greenland Brace

The modern Sculling for Support Stroke has its origins in the Sculling Support Brace practised by the Greenland Eskimos using their narrow unfeathered paddles. The sculling action of the extended blade was the same as for the modern Sculling for Support Stroke, but the angle the paddle made with the surface of the water was between 25° and 35°.

Greenland Brace

Fig. 7.11
Greenland Chest Scull or
Chest Brace

Fig. 7.12
Greenland Scull for
Support Stroke or
Vertical Support Stroke

Fig. 7.13
Greenland Front Scull or
Bow Scull or Front Brace

The paddle was held at face level. The knuckles of the paddler's hands faced rearwards, with the palms upwards. Both hands supported the underside of the nearest blade. As the kayak was tilted further over, the paddler would twist his body so that his chest and shoulders were parallel to the surface of the water, giving him added support. At the same time, the knuckles of the inboard or pivot hand would slide round the blade and rotate its grip forward through 180° to maintain the pivot. At this stage only the paddler's head would show above the water. (*See* fig. 7.11.)

As the reader progresses through this book it will become obvious that all traditional as well as modern rolling methods are based on three simple, basic manoeuvres. These are the Support Stroke/Brace, the Scull for Support Stroke, which I have already explained, and the Sweep Support Stroke, which is explained in chapter 9.

In the next stroke, the Vertical Scull, it is the continuous sweep of the correctly angled paddle blade in one direction only which provides sufficient lift to give the paddler support and prevent a capsize or brings the kayak upright again from the inverted position.

Vertical Scull

Vertical Scull

Fig. 7.14
Movement diagram showing the general direction of the paddle: surface view

Fig. 7.15
Position of the body during the sculling movement: fish-eye view

It is quite easy to bring a fully inverted, modern sea kayak upright after a capsize by sculling it to the surface using the paddle in the extended position, as you would for the Greenland Chest Scull (*see* fig. 7.11). Modern recreational sea kayaks are usually wider and a different shape than the traditional Inuit kayaks, and because of this they require more effort to right after a capsize. It is therefore important to have the paddle in the correct starting position.

Figure 7.14 shows the movement for the Vertical Scull with the stroke performed on the right-hand side of the body.

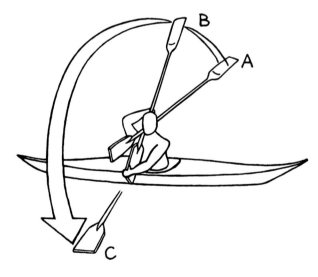

Fig. 7.14

Fig. 7.15

METHOD   **1** To get into the correct surface position, twist your body as far round to the right as you can so your upper body is at a right angle.

2 Hold the extended paddle so that it rests on your right shoulder. The extended outer blade should be as low down as possible – see position A in figure 7.14.

3 Grip the shaft with your right hand so your thumb is pointing down. Hook your left fingers over the top edge of the paddle blade near the tip.

4 Capsize over to the right. As you capsize your paddle may move into position B, as illustrated in figure 7.14. If it does, move it back to position A, the starting position.

5 Once you are upside-down, make sure your upper body stays at a right angle to the kayak, as described in point 1 above.

6 At this stage your upper paddle blade will be above the surface of the water and you can start sculling for support movement (*see* fig. 7.15). Figure 7.6 shows the position of the paddle blade and the direction of the stroke during this movement.

It is easy to become disorientated when you are upside-down and you may inadvertently move your body back into the normal forward-facing position. This is dangerous because the forward-facing position will point the paddle in the wrong direction and any further paddle movements will be ineffective.

To avoid this happening, first practise the correct paddle movement while standing on dry land as follows: stand upright, face forwards and place the paddle over your shoulder. Imagine the centre line of the kayak is running between your legs. Keeping your feet facing forwards, twist your body to the right so that your chest is at 90° to the centre line of the kayak. Bring the paddle over in a continuous sweep (compare this movement with The Headstand, fig. 23.1). Once you have mastered the sweeping movement you can incorporate the sculling movement in your practice.

Normally it doesn't really matter whether you twist your body sideways before or after you position the paddle on your shoulder, but it certainly did on one occasion for me: I was once asked to demonstrate the wind-up for this stroke when I was out on the water with a group of my coaching colleagues. The seas were short and steep and the wind was strong. As I positioned my body at right angles, the paddle was pointing to heaven. Next thing a blast of wind hit the extended blade and I suddenly found myself being blown over and capsizing backwards in the opposite direction of the stroke. I have never felt so confused. I forgot where I was and what I was supposed to be doing. All I could see was bubbles. I finally managed to sort myself out and reverted to the old tried-and-tested Pawlata Roll, which thankfully brought me to the surface amid gales of laughter from the onlookers and comments such as, 'Oh, so that's how it's done!'

INSTRUCTOR'S
NOTE

It is a good idea to have students begin their sculling movement when the paddle is in the most extended position over the shoulder, even though the paddle blade might flail about in the air for a few seconds before it hits the water.

However experienced a kayaker is, there will be times when capsize takes him or her totally by surprise. In such circumstances tried-and-tested techniques will usually avert disaster. **Graham Lyons**, *a keen white-water paddler and chairman of the BCU's National Coaching Committee, recalls the following capsize experience.*

I am not very keen on the sight of blood, particularly when it is my own! So I stayed in my seat, waiting for the doctor. However, curiosity eventually got the better of me and I walked over to the mirror above the sink. Some swelling on my left cheek was clearly visible and a tooth had been pushed through my lip. I opened my mouth, to find the remains of two shattered teeth.

What rankled was that, although the fall was graded at IV, I had done it several times before and I had not therefore been unduly apprehensive. In fact it would be a good test for the new kayak I was paddling – or so I thought!

As I approached the top, I knew that the line

was wrong but a quick sweep or so would put things right. The capsize was sudden and a total surprise. My first thought was one of annoyance. I was the last person down and the rest had managed it successfully. However a good roll was all that was needed to save my damaged pride. Instinctively, I set up for the roll and was just reminding myself that a good flick would be needed, when my hand hit a rock, pushing the paddle out of position. If the capsize had been a surprise, it was nothing to what happened next. A rock hit me in the side of the face with such tremendous force that it pushed my whole body backwards. There was no pain, but I knew that some teeth were broken because my mouth was full of little sharp splinters. I attempted another roll but it was weak and pathetic. The spirit had gone!

The next thing I knew was that I was standing knee-deep in the water, wiping blood away from my mouth. I watched my boat complete the rest of the rapid in rather better style than I had achieved so far.

CHAPTER 8 *Pawlata Roll*

We have an Austrian gentleman named H. W. Pawlata, known as Edi Pawlata, to thank for revolutionising the sport of kayaking. In 1927 and after studying the writings of Rasmussen, Nansen and Jophansen, he became the first man in Europe to perform an Eskimo Roll.

The roll which is named after him is generally thought to be the best to teach beginners. Most teachers would support this view because:

(a) it has the advantage of the leverage afforded by a paddle held in the extended position;
(b) there are several ways to teach the Pawlata Roll;
(c) it is a vital step in the progression towards the Screw Roll which is the most important roll of all.

The land drill method

Believe it or not, it is possible to learn the Pawlata Roll without getting wet. This may sound a bit far-fetched but it is possible. All that is required is that the paddler learns a simple land drill and then applies it underwater after a capsize. (See instructions on pp. 39–40.)

I would define a 'drill' as a certain number of preconceived arm and body movements, executed in the correct sequence and at exactly the right time. The drill is learned by repeating it time and time again until it becomes imprinted on the mind to such an extent that it can be repeated instantly and in whatever position the body may find itself.

As you practise the land drill, it may help you to imagine that you are sitting in a kayak rather than standing on firm ground. Find a space where waving the paddle about will not cause damage to property, any onlookers or the cat.

The drill sequence

Figs. 8.1–2 (continued over page)

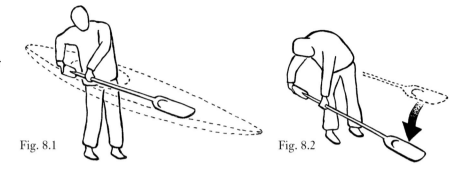

Fig. 8.1   Fig. 8.2

INSTRUCTIONS

1 Stand with your feet about a foot apart, both pointing forwards. Your feet are now pointing towards the imaginary bow of the imaginary kayak you imagine you are sitting in!

To complete the dry land roll on the left side, hold the paddle in the Extended Paddle Position.

(a) Without altering your hand grip in any way, move the paddle so that it is now pointing forwards along the right side of an imaginary kayak's deck. Your left wrist will now be in an uncomfortable position with the knuckles pointing outwards.

(b) Your right hand is gripping the top corner of the now vertical paddle blade. Your thumb is pointing down, the knuckles towards the rear.

(c) The outside edge of the foremost blade is angled slightly towards the ground. The driving face is upwards.

(d) The arms should not be straight but bent at slightly more than a right angle.

(e) You are still facing and leaning slightly forwards.

This is the preliminary position adopted immediately prior to the start of the Pawlata Roll. It is referred to as the wind-up (pronounced wined-up), and this would be the posture you would adopt if you were sitting in a kayak on the surface preparing to capsize and roll. (*See* fig. 8.1.)

Although you are in fact standing during this drill, your upper body movements and arm movements will be exactly as they would be if you were sitting.

Because I cannot ask you to stand on your head, and because few of us have the sort of friends who are prepared to hold us upside-down while we crack them about the head and shins with our flailing paddle, I ask you now to IMAGINE you are upside-down. Imagine that the sky is now the bottom of the pool, and that the surface of the water is on a plane around you, roughly level with your knees.

Figs 8.3–9
The drill sequence
continued

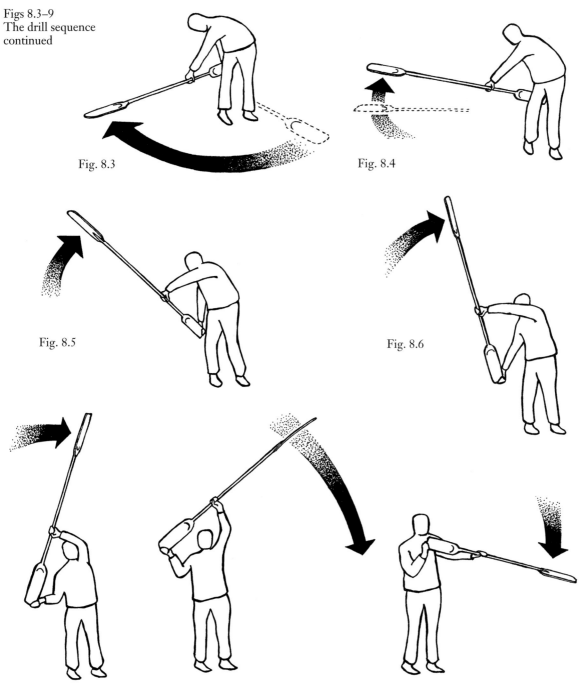

Fig. 8.3

Fig. 8.4

Fig. 8.5

Fig. 8.6

Fig. 8.7

Fig. 8.8

Fig 8.9

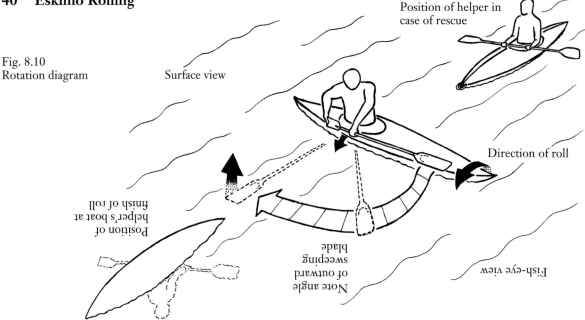

Fig. 8.10
Rotation diagram

Position of helper in
case of rescue

Surface view

Direction of roll

Position of
helper's boat at
finish of roll

Note angle
of outward
sweeping
blade

Fish-eye view

If all this sounds impossibly and unnecessarily confusing then forget it. Just learn the drill! Be assured that when you ARE upside-down in the water, the drill will work and it will bring you back to the surface.

2 Now for the actual movement. Without shifting your feet, twist your body outwards and down from the waist on the paddle side. Straighten your arms and push the paddle to a position about knee level (the paddle is still parallel to the ground). (*See* fig. 8.2.)

3 With a straight left arm, sweep the extended blade out to your right side, till it is at right angles to your feet. During this sweep out, the paddle blade must stay parallel to the ground and the angle of the extended blade remain the same. Your right hand should have pushed the nearest paddle blade forwards while doing this. (*See* fig. 8.3.)

4 As the right hand pushes down slightly on the paddle blade, pull the extended blade over your head with the left hand, reaching out and up as far as possible with a straight LEFT arm, in an arc of 180°. Finish up with the paddle at right angles to your feet on the left side (*see* figs 8.4–9). During the sweep overhead, the bicep of the left arm should have brushed past your nose (*see* fig. 8.6).

Although this drill is taught as a series of separate movements, the finished sequence is one dynamic movement in which each part merges

The Pawlata is one of the easiest rolls for novices to learn. In this photograph, 15-year-old Paul Hutchinson completes his very first roll. After a few seconds of stunned silence, he summed it all up with, 'How about that then!' Although the kayak he is using is a short white-water kayak beloved of waterfall jumpers, its rounded ends make it ideal for swimming pool use. PHOTO: DEREK C. HUTCHINSON

The author during a rolling demonstration at one of L. L. Bean's sea kayak symposiums. Frozen by the camera, the plume of water around the head captures the movement and speed of the roll. Note the paddle held in the normal paddling position for the Reverse Screw Roll. PHOTO COURTESY DEREK C. HUTCHINSON.

with the next. The whole drill should take about three seconds. Start counting as you start the first trunk movement – 'One thousand and one'. Sweep out – 'One thousand and two', and pull over – 'One thousand and three'.

It will help to recite the drill:

WIND-UP	Wind-up position, grip must be right,
PUSH DOWN	Head and arms up to the light,
SWEEP OUT	Sweep out to the side, level as she goes,
PULL OVER	Pull over the head, biceps on nose.

Tom Caskey, *a BCU coach who has accompanied the author on both his North Sea crossing attempts, describes his first real experience of a Pawlata Roll.*

I hadn't been paddling very long. I had done a couple of weekend courses with the kids from the school but they were just as inexperienced as I was. On this occasion I had taken a group of young people to the Catton Outdoor Centre and it was towards the end of the week, on the Friday lunchtime, that I reminded the resident instructor that he had promised to teach me to roll. We drove to a spot on the River Tyne, near Tyne Green where the water is always still. It was there he got down to the job. The water was cold. He would stand beside me and after about an hour or so, I think I did manage to get upright, but only occasionally, in the straight extended Pawlata position. This was to be the sum total of my roll training.

It was not long after this that I started to do a fair bit of paddling on my own, off the Northumberland coast. On this particular day, I was paddling close in shore, up from Seahouses towards the Coastguard station.

I was paddling, unconcerned, about 300 yards from the shore when I saw this big curling wave heading in. I decided I'd better try and paddle out of its way. As I turned, I saw another wave approaching at an angle to it. I hadn't been out in breaking waves before so I reckoned that the only thing to do was to head out between them. The waves had started to curl and I paddled hell-for-leather for the apex between them. Now I reckon these waves were about seven feet tall. When I hit them I was stopped dead. I felt myself moving backwards and I must have done a couple of back loops – i.e. over the top a couple of times. As I was being tumbled about in this massive water, I thought I was going to be dragged out of the boat. I decided this was my big chance and I was going to have to roll! I can still remember the feeling. Surprisingly, my mind wasn't in a turmoil. I suppose I was out of breath but I thought to myself, 'The main thing this time is that it's got to work!'

I got myself into the rolling position for the Pawlata. I think I just pushed the paddle outwards. I don't feel I did anything else. The next thing I knew, I was on the surface. I had gone through the motions of doing a roll but it was the water that had brought me upright.

CHAPTER 9 *Sweep Support Stroke*

Some people find that they cannot apply the drill for the Pawlata Roll when the time comes to actually do it. The trouble is that they suddenly try to work out the mechanics of the movement when they are hanging upside down, with the result that the paddle shoots out on the opposite side to that which has been so carefully practised.

There is an alternative method for teaching yourself the Pawlata Roll. To do this, you should find some sheltered water that has a shallow shelving bottom. Begin by getting used to the feel of cold water on your hot head. Do this by holding on to the bow loop or toggle of a friend's kayak and dipping your head completely under the water. After this, try a couple of practice Eskimo bow rescues. This will boost your confidence and help build up a rapport between you and your rescuer.

Position yourself in shallow water about two-feet deep. Place your paddle out on the left side in the Extended Paddle Position, but make sure it is touching the bottom. With this support, lean over until you can flick yourself up when your ear is touching the water.

Now practise the Sweep Support Stroke in water about two- to three-feet deep.

Method

1   The paddler adopts the wind-up position. From there the paddle is lifted over so that the driving face is in a position ready to be placed on the surface of the water. (*See* fig. 9.1.)

2   The driving face is now angled downwards. As the blade is placed on the water, the paddler leans over to the left – gently at first – at the same time striking the driving face of the paddle downwards and outwards with its leading edge high. (*See* fig. 9.2.)

3   The blade will plane across the surface of the water supporting your weight all the way. (*See* fig. 9.3.)

Fig. 9.1   Fig. 9.2   Fig. 9.3

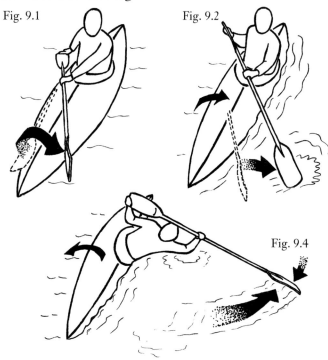

Fig. 9.4

Sweep Support Stroke

Figs 9.1–4 The stroke cycle

Fig. 9.5
Movement diagram: fish-eye view

4 The farthest point of the lean should be when the paddle is at right angles to the hull. At this point, the kayak is hip-flicked upright again. (*See* fig. 9.4.)

If the Sweep for Support Stroke fails, simply right yourself by pushing off the bottom. You may find the paddle suddenly starts to fight back and wraps itself awkwardly around your neck, in which case release your grip and signal to your helper that you need a rescue. If, however, you are living dangerously and trying all this alone and unaided, then swim the kayak into the shallows until you feel your hands touch the bottom.

With practice, it should not be long before it is possible for you to return to the surface after allowing yourself to hang completely upside-down. (*See* fig. 9.5.) This is a half roll. All that needs to be done now is to capsize on the opposite side and come up on the other.

For me, **Mike Jones** *was a hero. As far as I am concerned, he was the finest white-water river expeditionary kayak paddler I have ever had the privilege to meet. In the summer of 1978, Mike was tragically killed on the Braldu River in Pakistan, while attempting to save a friend's life. The following extracts from his book,* Canoeing Down Everest *(Hodder & Stoughton, 1979), paint an incredible word-picture of what it is like to paddle and roll while fighting for survival in Class VI rapids.*

A canoeist sits in his craft with his legs stuck straight out in front of him at right angles, his head is only just above the water level and his face is constantly covered with spray. His angle of vision is very low, yet he must try to see what lies ahead as he hurtles down at over 30 miles an hour, interpret the best channel to take and estimate how steep a rapid is, how much water there will be in the shallower parts, where he can 'break-out' of a counter-current or where he can slide into the bank for a breather. All this requires split-second judgement and timing which is most exhausting at high altitude, for the lack of oxygen slows the thinking speed right down. He cannot see over giant boulders but must swing round them with his paddle whirling, hoping nothing alarming lies beyond. All the time he is being swept along he must try to maintain his balance, keep the canoe upright, and keep it going forwards and not get twisted round in eddies so that he is facing backwards and cannot see what lies ahead. Even one Eskimo Roll in rough water here would be exhausting because it was hard enough to get air into the lungs when right side up, but to be submerged for several minutes in such icy water, unable to breathe, would be excruciatingly painful. Two Eskimo Rolls in quick succession would clearly be dangerous.

'A trial run on the Dudh Kosi, Pakistan'

I ride wave after wave using the few seconds the canoe* is on the crest of the wave to alter direction. Edge to the left to miss a stopper, to the right to miss a partly submerged rock. In front, Mick goes over and I try to keep an eye on him whilst trying to slow the canoe down and get a line on the rapids. A wave crashes down on top of me, and then another and I drop into a stopper. I brace hard on the face of it and paddle along the wall of white water until, after what seems like a lifetime, I finally find a run out.

Mick seems to be in trouble and suddenly his canoe stands vertically in the water and he loops in a stopper. I lean hard over and try and edge the canoe away but the water is too heavy and the canoe fails to respond, as Mick's canoe comes crashing down on top of me. And then I'm over. No time for fear. No time to get a breath of air. The cold is intense and automatically the paddles go into the Eskimo Roll position, a sweep, a press and the canoe rights itself.

The canoe bucketed madly down a series of waves, crawling to the top and then accelerating as it went down the other side. On my right a giant curling wave came screaming in and I braced madly as it crashed down on top of me. I felt the boat submerging and grabbed a lungful of air before going over in the ice cold water. It is a strange frightening world being swept along out of control at over 30 miles an hour. There is no more thundering noise, just murky, swirling water in this crazy, topsy-turvy world of the capsized canoeist. Mechanically the

*In these extracts, Mike Jones uses the generic term 'canoe' for a white-water kayak.

paddles go into place, sweep around and I lever the canoe upright, rapidly clear my eyes and decide on a line down the next section of river.

We were still two miles above Ghat and by 3 p.m., cold and exhausted by eight hours canoeing, we arrived at the last rapid we would shoot before leaving the canoes on the bank and dropping down to the camp site. It consisted of two large ten-foot-high waterfalls, separated by a section of 30 feet or so of broken water.

Mick shot it on the left, I bumbled through on the right and Rob set off to go down the centre. We watched horrified as he was caught in a stopper above the first fall and capsized. There was no time to roll and his canoe was swept upside-down over the first ten-foot drop, and within a few seconds over the second. We felt helpless as the canoe cleared the stopper at the bottom of the fall and crunched into a rock. Panic gripped me momentarily as I imagined that Rob had been swept out of the boat and was swimming, and then to my relief a paddle appeared and Rob rolled the canoe upright, with no more than a series of deep scratches on his crash helmet where he had been crashed against submerged rocks.

It had been a lucky escape, as Rob told us afterwards. He realised when he went over at the top of the first fall that he did not have time to roll up before the second one so he had just wedged himself into the canoe as tightly as possible and held his breath as he went over both.

The following incident occurred during a training session on the River Inn, one of Europe's wildest rivers.

John came through first. He took a bold line down the centre of the rapid, edged two big stoppers at the top and was thrown sideways by the final stopper before the chute. With a few well-timed back strokes he managed to reverse the canoe off the left-hand rock guarding the entrance to the chute and was swept over and down the chute broadside on, capsizing but rolling up effortlessly as he cleared the bottom stopper.

Mick Hopkinson did not fare quite so well. He capsized shortly after he hit the first stopper, failed on his first attempt to roll and barely succeeded on his second. I watched horrified as he was swept against the large rock which John had so narrowly missed and dropped the camera as he was wedged broadside on the rock and swept underneath. It was exactly the same situation in which two Germans had drowned in 1968. I felt completely helpless as I raced along my rocky ledge up to a point directly opposite where Mick had disappeared. There was no sign of either Mick or the canoe as I desperately scanned the roaring waterfall. Roger Huyton, upstream of my position, began shouting and gesticulating madly and as I jerked around, Mick reappeared on the far side of the rock, still in his canoe, having survived being swept and trapped underneath the rock, his helmet twisted, and the spray-sheet ripped half off. He was about to drop over an eight-foot vertical waterfall. Amazingly he managed to straighten the canoe and leaning back along the stern deck, he nose-dived into the splash pool beneath, capsized and rolled up looking somewhat the worse for wear.

CHAPTER 10 *How to teach the Pawlata Roll*

The student should have completed the necessary confidence exercises, e.g. Capsize Drill, swimming with the kayak, and the Hip Flick. It is a good idea for the pupil to go through the land drill three or four times, so that he becomes familiar with the direction in which his limbs are supposed to be moving.

First stage

1 The pupil adopts the wind-up position (*see* fig. 10.1). As the instructor, you will place yourself at the bow of the boat so that you can make sure the paddle is at the correct angle (outside edge angled down towards the water).

Learning with assistance

Fig. 10.1
Position of the instructor
before the roll

2 Explain what is going to happen in the following way:

'When I tell you, I want you to capsize. I shall hold the paddle in position on the deck until you are completely upside down. I shall then quickly slap the paddle blade on the surface of the water a couple of times to give you the feel of where the surface is situated. I shall then move the paddle out to the side. As soon as you feel the paddle is out at right angles to you, pull yourself up as you did in the support stroke exercises.'

Fig. 10.2
Ready to roll:
signal to capsize

Fig. 10.3
Controlling the direction
of the paddle

Your last words to the pupil should be:

'Do not think about what I am going to do, all YOU have to do is just relax and let ME do it all. All YOU have to do is pull up when the paddle gets into position.'

3 Before giving the signal to capsize, make sure your pupil is seated comfortably with knees wedged under the cockpit coaming, nose-clip in position.

4 Reach underneath the bow of the kayak, take hold of the paddle and the boat as shown in figure 10.2. Give the signal to capsize.

5 As soon as your pupil is upside-down, quickly lift his blade a couple of inches above the water and slap it down smartly on to the surface. Now move the blade out to the side across the surface, its leading edge high.

At this stage you may find that, despite all your guidance, the pupil has decided to think for himself whilst underwater. He will therefore have either become mentally frozen, in which case the paddle will be held in the grip of death rigidly against the side of the boat or it will try and take off on the wrong side. This, of course, is why you are holding the paddle in the manner shown, so that you are able to control the direction of the paddle and push it and the boat apart (*see* fig. 10.3).

On the first attempt you may also find that the roller tries to pull to the surface before the paddle has been positioned at right angles.

At one time I would take hold of the paddle with both hands and attempt to walk out to the side, thinking that all I had to do was guide the blade, only to find the kayak was following the paddle. If the pupil does not relax (after the initial outward movement) you may have to use your foot to help continue the paddle's movement away from the side of the boat (*see* fig. 10.4).

The student must practise until you FEEL by the tensions and tugs as you hold the paddle that he now instinctively knows the direction of the outward sweeping blade and can pull himself upright with your help. Once you are satisfied, move on to the next stage.

Fig. 10.4
Using the foot to control
the paddle movement

Fig. 10.5
Partial assistance in shallow water

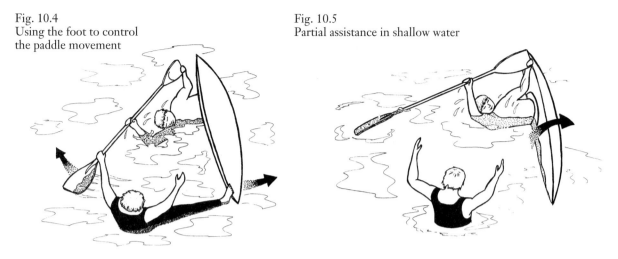

Partial assistance

IN SHALLOW
WATER

The pupil is sitting ready in the correct wind-up position. You then explain what you are going to do:

> 'If you do not open your eyes, now is the time to start so that you can watch the direction of the paddle. On my signal you will capsize as before. I will wait a couple of seconds while you become orientated, then I shall move your paddle out about a foot from the side of the boat and back again a couple of times. This will give you the "feel" of the position of the paddle and the direction in which you are going to move it . . . any questions?'

Once you feel all this has been grasped, position yourself and your hands as before, and give the signal to capsize. Once the student is upside-down, move the paddle as you said you would and then stand clear. If all goes well the paddle should move out along the surface into the position where the pupil can pull himself upright (*see* fig. 10.5). Of course, at the last minute things can go wrong – in which case be ready to step in and help raise him to the surface.

Once this stage has been completed successfully, in that it has been repeated several times to your satisfaction, the big moment has now arrived for the solo attempt.

IN DEEP WATER

It may not always be practical for the instructor to stand next to the pupil. Perhaps the water is cold and the helper has no protective clothing. If such is the case, the instructor can give partial assistance in deeper water from the comfort of his own kayak (*see* figs 10.6, 10.7, 10.8).

In the event of a failed roll, instead of pulling the pupil up by hand, the instructor will give assistance with an Eskimo Rescue.

It takes practice for an instructor to become proficient using this deep-water teaching method. It necessarily follows that many of the confidence exercises should be practised by both teacher and pupil afloat together.

The solo attempt

By this time your protégé should be bursting with the confidence of success bolstered by his newly discovered courage. This is just about the time when mistakes occur, so while your pupil is sitting ready in the wind-up position and raring to go, take time to give some important new advice and a few reminders. The first point is very important:

> 'Up until now I have held on to your paddle blade until you were upside-down. In this way it was in the correct position for the outward sweep. When you capsize alone, however, the act of rolling over will dislodge the carefully placed extended paddle blade to a position about one foot from the deck and thus nearer the bottom. The first thing you must do after the capsize therefore is to *open your eyes and place the paddle back again into its starting position.*'

After checking to make sure that the wind-up is correct, give another reminder:

> 'Don't forget that the biceps of the foremost arm must brush past your nose as you pull the paddle over your head.'

Once you are sure that your advice has been absorbed, direct your pupil to retire out of your reach – a few yards will be sufficient – then give him the signal to capsize. He will now perform what we all hope will be a perfect first-time Eskimo Roll. If your luck is anything like mine, however, the pupil will make some tiny, hardly significant mistake which will cause the whole roll to fail and in so doing turn your wide-eyed hopeful into a human being filled with despondency and fail-ure. This is quite normal and at this time you must call upon your reserves of patience and sympathy. More important, however, is that any mistakes should be spotted immediately and corrected, so that what starts off as a small error is not consolidated into a bad habit. It is no

Partial assistance in deep water

Fig. 10.6
Partially assisted roll in deep water: the instructor holds the paddle in place during the wind-up

Fig. 10.7
Controlling the direction of the paddle

Fig. 10.8
During the outward sweep, the instructor pushes the kayak away

good merely saying 'Try again!' The error must be pointed out and corrected straight away.

As the teacher, your first concern is to make sure that your student is in the correct wind-up position. This is the time when most rolling problems start, so check the following:

(a) rear hand on top of blade;
(b) front hand with knuckes bent outwards – wrist up;
(c) elbows bent;
(d) front blade angle.

Common faults

Figures 10.9–10.13 show some of the more common mistakes which you are likely to encounter.

Fig. 10.9   During the wind-up the TOP corner of the paddle blade should be held snug in the palm of the hand. It is worth mentioning that some books teach a handgrip elsewhere on the blade. Well, why not try this simple test. First kneel down and hold the paddle in the Extended Paddle Position. Now lean over so that your weight is totally supported by the paddle on the ground. Relax so that your fingers open. The blade is now supported by your open palm. Kneel upright again and this time hold the blade in one of the positions marked with a cross.

Hold the paddle tight and then lean over again until you are completely committed to the support it gives. Now relax the hand that is holding the blade and take note of what happens. (Don't worry, the bleeding will soon stop and with any luck your elbow isn't fractured.)

Fig. 10.10   This shows the result of another error in the wind-up position. The blade shown planes out on or near the surface, so as to be as high as possible for the downward pull to the

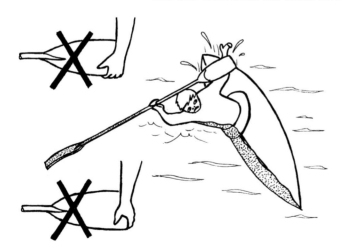

Fig. 10.9
Fault: incorrect grip on paddle blade during wind-up

Fig. 10.10
Fault: extended paddle blade held at incorrect angle, which will cause the paddle to sink during the outward sweep

Fig. 10.11
Fault: paddle pulled down before the outward sweep

surface. If the take-off angle is a downward one, it will place the paddle in a position that will make the roll either difficult or impossible.

Encourage your student to 'feel' the angle of the extended blade by the outward tilt of the held paddle blade.

Fig. 10.11 The student has forgotten to move the paddle out to the side before the downward pull. This is a non-roll. Go back to the exercise shown in figure 10.3.

Fig. 10.12 Everything has started well but the student has become impatient and is trying to roll up before the paddle is as far out as it will go. Pulling the kayak to the surface will be difficult. The student should be reminded that he must feel the biceps of the outward sweeping arm brush past his nose. This will place the paddle out at right angles.

If the student finds this difficult, as an alternative he can be told to throw his body backwards towards the rear deck, at the same time as the paddle is out, as far as it will go. He should then find the paddle automatically arriving into an acceptable rolling position. This will result in what is known as a lay-back roll. Quite a number of people choose this as their rolling position, but it must be remembered that when rolling over rocks or in white water, the front of the paddler's face will not be protected. (*See* p. 54.)

Fig. 10.13 If the paddle is not pushed up to the surface, the held blade will become trapped behind the roller's back, preventing an outward sweep. Remind the student: 'Push up towards the light!' (*See* p. 54).

Fig. 10.12
Fault: paddle pulled down before completion of the outward sweep

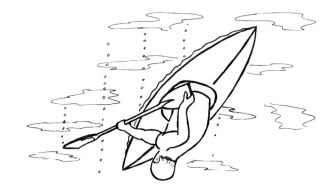

Fig. 10.13
Fault: paddle blade trapped behind paddler's back because the hands are not pushed to the surface (fish-eye view)

Bob Licht *was once a keen white-water paddler and river rafter. He has now transferred his interest to the sea and is currently the owner of 'Sea Trek' which has become the largest school for sea kayaking in North America. His story indicates the importance of knowing the right procedures when out on the water with a kayak.*

It was one of those beautiful days in the Bay Area when you think that nothing can go wrong. Things were going just fine until we were crossing Racoon Strait. It was then that the double in the group capsized. Once the occupants hit the water they really panicked. I paddled close up to them to give some help but they immediately grabbed hold of my kayak and tried to climb up on to it. This flipped me over, so I went into a roll that I knew would bring me straight up again. It didn't work! I couldn't think what was wrong – so I tried again with more effort than before. I *still* couldn't get up! I couldn't think what was the matter – until I realised that two people were still hanging on to my boat. It was then that I felt my specs slipping off. Somehow I managed to hold them in my teeth.

I tried to roll up again, but failed. By this time I really needed some air. I knew that if I could just roll high enough to clear my face, I could get a quick breath. But with my specs stuck in my teeth, I couldn't open my mouth. I was now faced with a dilemma. If I wanted air, I had to open my mouth. I knew that if I opened my mouth I would lose my spectacles. I decided that the air was more important. As I pulled myself up to the surface for the third time, I opened my mouth and got the air I needed. I remember thinking, 'God! These two are slow learners – they've still got hold of me!' It was about then that they must have finally realised that if they didn't let go of my boat, I wasn't going to get up. Once they finally let go of me, I rolled up, no problem – but without my specs. However, they do say that if you know where something is, it's not lost!

CHAPTER 11 *Follow-up exercises*

Once you can wind-up and capsize on one side, then rise to the surface on the other, you can be justly proud and congratulate yourself on your newly acquired skill. However, your skill level so far is not such that it could be guaranteed to right you after an accidental capsize.

Up until this point, you have been able to prepare yourself psychologically for the capsize, and have had enough time to tune in to the required wind-up drill. You must aim to be able to roll instinctively, bearing in mind that when you do capsize, you may be on the move, short of breath and the elements may well be anything but conducive to calm, controlled thinking.

Exercises

To help you to gain the confidence necessary to arrive at the sublime state of being a genuine 'first-time roller', you should practise the following exercises:

1 Place the paddle on the water so that it floats next to the kayak on your wind-up side. Capsize on that side, taking hold of the paddle as you go over. Your front hand will probably grab the shaft in the normal wind-up position but you will have to grope for a second or two to complete the wind-up before rolling to the surface.

2 Hold the paddle in the normal paddling position and then capsize. You will now have to keep cool and adopt the wind-up position while hanging upside-down. Once you can roll like this, give yourself a further pat on the back.

3 Throw the paddle so that it floats parallel to the kayak, still on your wind-up side but about five or six feet away. Capsize and swim the kayak to the paddle. Take hold of it carefully, wind-up and then roll up. Award yourself several pats on the back. You are now ready to move on to the most important roll of all. This is the Screw Roll – so called because when the roll is performed on the move, the kayak appears to screw itself through the water.

Peter Knowles *is a well-known white-water expedition paddler, with many first descents to his credit. The following capsize experience is one that he remembers very well.*

It happened on one of the early trips down the Grand Canyon in 1973. We had done all the big drops like Crystal and Lava but we'd really got into surfing some of the big rapids. I was surfing this big green wave that stretched across the river, which was part of one of the larger rapids. A few of the lads had tried to catch it before me but they didn't seem to have quite enough speed. Anyhow, I eventually managed to get on to this wave. Meanwhile the rest of the party got miles in front of me. The next thing I knew, this great black thing, like a wall towering over me came up from behind. I realised it was one of those big motorised rafts – they're about 35 feet long, made up of three bridging pontoons lashed side by side – on its way down the river. The fellow driving this thing hadn't seen me because I was down in the trough of the wave and I hadn't seen him because I couldn't see behind, over the wave. So the first thing I knew was this great big black wall of rubber just about to hit me.

I did a bit of high-speed thinking! I decided to capsize and let it pass over me and then roll up. I just managed to get half a breath of air before rolling over. It was then I thought of the big 60 hp Johnson that they have fastened to the back to help steer and drive these contraptions through the water. I had this vision of the prop making mincemeat out of me. I was upside-down in all this froth and stuff, when I realised my kayak had become jammed between the chains that lash the pontoons together to form this big raft. So there I was, stuck upside-down underneath this raft, amongst all these chains going down one of the rapids on the Grand Canyon.

My mind eventually started to work. I had this 60 hp motor waiting for me if I happened to pop out at the back so I thought I'd better get out of the boat quick. I was short of air so I bailed out and I started to claw and clamber my way through this underwater obstacle course of chains and stuff, until I got to what I thought was the side of the raft . . . but it wasn't. I expected to get a big gulp of air but I'd only reached where the two pontoons were joined together. I had another panic-stricken eight feet or so of the obstacle course to get me to the outside edge. By this time, I was pretty far gone. I remember putting my arm up. Luckily some tourist on the raft saw this arm waving about, grabbed it and pulled me in.

The helmsman of the raft was white as a sheet. I think he was almost in a worse state than I was because he thought he'd run me down and drowned me. Mind you . . . he damn nearly had done!

CHAPTER 12

Screw Roll and Short Pawlata Roll

You will find that the Screw Roll is the most useful roll of all. Most competent rollers choose it as their 'instinctive' roll and the reason is simple. The hand grip never moves from the normal paddle position. Let's be realistic: no one wants to start fumbling about under swirling water in order to move hands and paddle into a completely different position.

In the Screw Roll, the direction and manner in which the paddle moves is the same as for the Pawlata Roll, so no new skills need to be learned. However, because the leverage is shorter, it is important to have a good Hip Flick and to place the paddle correctly. It is the rear wrist of the hand holding the shaft which controls the angle of the sweeping blade.

Short Pawlata Roll

There is an exercise which will help you make an easy transition from the Pawlata Roll to the Screw Roll. I shall call this the 'Short Pawlata'.

ROLLING METHOD   **1** Hold the paddle in the position shown in figure 12.1. The rear hand holds the paddle at the point where the blade joins the shaft. You will feel the edge of the blade pressed against the side of your hand and in this way it is possible to be aware of the angle of the front blade.

Fig. 12.1
Hold the shaft at the throat
for a Short Pawlata Roll

2 During the roll it is important to push the rear hand as high as possible so that the blade clears the upturned hull (*see* figs 12.3 and 12.6).

3 The Hip Flick and body lean are vital ingredients to a successful roll. Whether the paddler leans forwards with the head tucked in or lies along the back deck is a matter of personal preference. As I have said before, though, leaning back exposes the face and neck, and this could prove dangerous if a roll is attempted in shallow rapids or over underwater obstacles. The most important consideration, however, is to get to the surface.

Screw Roll

Once the Short Pawlata has been mastered, the Screw Roll is a direct progression, and it is this roll which should be your first plan of action after a capsize. Practise the roll wearing normal paddling clothing, e.g. personal buoyancy and crash helmet. Some people find that wearing a life-jacket (Personal Flotation Device or PFD) helps to bring them to the surface before starting the roll, while others prefer the buoyancy provided by a wet-suit top.

Practise rolling on both sides. This is perhaps more important on rivers, when speed is often essential, than it is on the sea.

If you capsize during an energetic paddle down a rapid you could find yourself short of breath. Paddling in and out through surf will have a similar effect. It is a good idea to practise rolling after short sprints or at times when you feel out of breath. Remember that fear and anxiety affect your respiration. It is important, therefore, to KEEP CALM.

Screw Roll

Fig. 12.2
Surface wind-up position

Fig. 12.3
Movement diagram: fish-eye view

Fig. 12.2

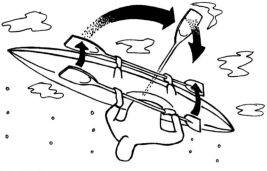

Fig. 12.3

John Abbenhouse and Bob Licht screw-rolling a Seascape double kayak on Lake Michigan during the Great Lakes Sea Kayak Symposium held at Travers City. The two men went on to bring the kayak up with a well-timed Hand Roll, much to the delight of the admiring onlookers. Photo courtesy: John Abbenhouse

ROLLING METHOD

Let us take a typical situation. You are paddling down a rapid river. It has taken some effort to punch your way through the stoppers and haystacks of water. You are puffing and blowing as you drop down into a particularly nasty hole. Suddenly you feel yourself going over. In the split second before you hit the water, try to take a gulp of air. All is now bubbles and confusion.

1   Twist your shoulders through 90° so that the paddle shaft is parallel to the side of the boat.

2   Push your arms and the paddle up towards the light – head forwards, almost touching the deck. Make sure that the extended blade is horizontal and so parallel to the surface of the water.

3   With a final twist to make sure that the leading edge is high, make the outward sweep.

4   As you do this, throw your body back along the rear deck. The back of your head should touch the deck. If you are rolling on your right side, you will feel your left foot exert pressure against the footrest.

5   Pull sharply down with your outward hand and Hip Flick to the surface. Your paddle should now be in a position to continue the forward paddling stroke.

OF COURSE, YOU MAY FAIL. Keep calm! With any luck you might have been able to snatch a quick breath on the way down. Quickly slide your hands along into the Short Pawlata position; this will ensure that the paddle blade is at the correct angle and you now have more leverage . . . Roll up!

White water is full of froth and air bubbles which give a much reduced support to the downward striking paddle blade. To compensate for this, a good powerful Hip Flick will be needed to bring the kayak to the surface, regardless of how hard you pull down on the paddle.

STAGES OF THE SCREW ROLL

The seven stages of the Screw Roll are shown with the rear view in figures 12.4–12.10. To execute a lay-back recovery (*see* fig. 12.10) the body should be thrown backwards along the rear deck during the downward strike and Hip Flick (*see* fig. 12.8). Some people find this easier than leaning forwards.

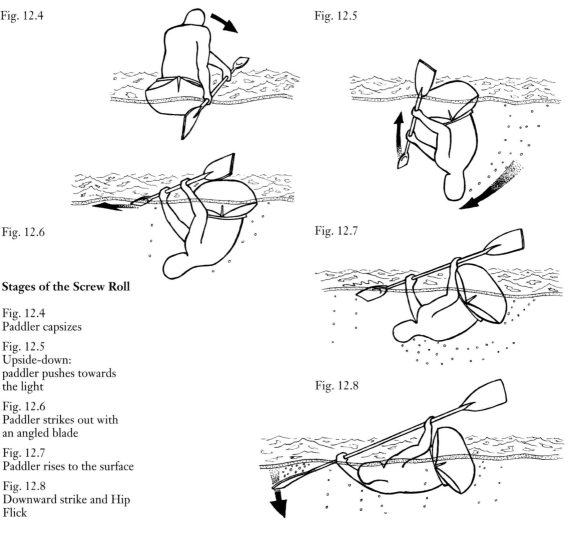

Fig. 12.4

Fig. 12.5

Fig. 12.6

Fig. 12.7

Fig. 12.8

Stages of the Screw Roll

Fig. 12.4
Paddler capsizes

Fig. 12.5
Upside-down:
paddler pushes towards
the light

Fig. 12.6
Paddler strikes out with
an angled blade

Fig. 12.7
Paddler rises to the surface

Fig. 12.8
Downward strike and Hip
Flick

**Stages of the Screw Roll,
continued**

Fig. 12.9
Upright recovery, leaning
forwards

Fig. 12.10
Lay-back recovery

Fig. 12.9

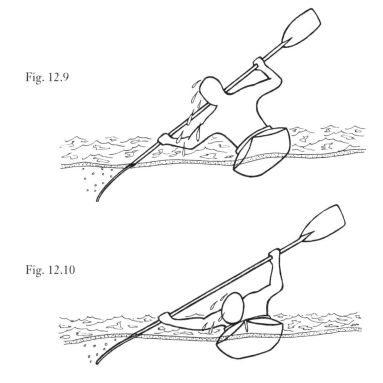

Fig. 12.10

Using a white-water kayak,
the author returns to the
surface after a Screw Roll.
White-water kayaks that
have pointed ends are not
really suitable for practice in
a swimming pool. If you
have to use one in a
swimming pool, it should
only be used for stationary
rolling practice where it
cannot cause injury;
it should not be used for
practising strokes, paddling
around, and certainly not
for pool polo. Photo
courtesy Derek C.
Hutchinson

Martin Meling, *who teaches kayaking and navigation and who paddles extensively on the sea, recalls a Screw Roll during a trip down Warden Gorge.*

I was with a group of others paddling down the North Tyne. I'd been down a number of times so there was no problem. When we reached Warden Gorge, it was decided that, being one of the leaders, I would go down first. The other man, the coach in charge, would bring up the rear.

Warden Gorge is graded 3 to 4 but I was familiar with the route down. Everything was going fine until I came to this little drop. It was only about three feet. Anyhow I went over and capsized at the bottom. I couldn't believe it. The cold water hit me so I went for a Screw Roll. I seemed to get halfway up, then I went down again. This was terrible, so I slid my hand along the loom until I felt the blade and I tried again. The same thing happened – I got halfway then I went down again. I thought, 'That's it!' and bailed out. I felt so humiliated. I just sat on the bank and watched the others come down. Nobody else seemed to have any problem. I felt awful. I wondered what Lofty would think of me. Then I thought perhaps he wouldn't say anything and that would make me feel worse.

He was the last to come down and I watched him reach the tiny fall. Then at the bottom he capsized too. I couldn't believe it. I saw his paddle sweep out for a roll but he failed to come up and he had to try again. Then he failed again and had to come out. He looked quite shocked and he started to tow his kayak towards the bank where I was sitting. My spirits rose and I remember I felt very much better.

These clever rear-view photographs of 14-year-old Dominic Kaines screw-rolling an Orion sea kayak were taken at the moment of the all-important Hip Flick. In this lay-back recovery (*left*) his head leaves the water last of all. He is using a modern 'Toksook' paddle, a design based on the paddles used by the Eskimos of the Kotzebue region of Alaska.
PHOTOS: STEVE DORRITY

CHAPTER 13 Reverse Screw Roll

Sometimes called the Short Steyr Roll, the Reverse Screw is the most useful of all lean-back rolls. Because the hands remain in the normal paddling position, it is directly linked to the Screw Roll, and indeed it can be considered an alternative to the latter. Although I do not recommend it, due to the risk of face injury, a number of white-water river paddlers seem to favour the Reverse Screw as their first choice rolling method.

The wind-up

During the wind-up the head should almost touch the rear deck with the paddle held as shown in figure 13.1. Twisting the rear blade so that the driving face is angled outwards will feel awkward, but it will be more comfortable as the roll progresses.

Rolling method

1 Once upside-down (*see* fig. 13.2), twist your body up towards the light.

2 Push the paddle towards the surface and sweep the rear blade forwards. You will find that the hands unwind naturally until the paddle is at right angles.

3 Once the paddle gets into this position, pull down and Hip Flick to the surface.

A surface view showing the position of the hands in relation to the upper blade is given in figure 13.3.

When correctly executed this roll demands very little effort. During the first attempts, however, many people tend to sweep the rear blade too far forwards. They then find that they must change direction and sweep the blade back towards the rear again into the more familiar finishing position of the Screw Roll.

Fig. 13.1
Surface wind-up position

Fig. 13.2
Movement diagram:
fish-eye view

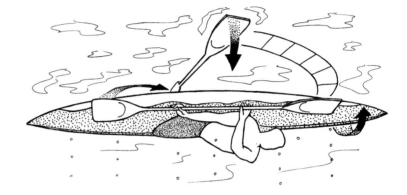

Fig. 13.3
Surface view of the paddle
movement, seen from the
rear

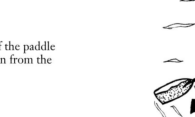

bow

stern

John Chamberlin *is an experienced sea-kayaker, with several first crossings to his credit, including two of the Irish Sea. As vice president of the Midland Canoe Club, he remembers a practice session at a local school pool during which the chill of the day was swept away by a couple performing the Screw Roll.*

Members of the Midland Canoe Club, some shivering in the cooled air, stood around the sides of Repton School's open-air pool, its surface ruffled by the light evening breeze.

The club's new Canadian Canoe – it was a KW Strike C2 – was launched and its nouveau crew powered it confidently across the water, preparing for its first official practice roll, determined that the oft-discussed theory would result in a first-time success.

The principle was simple enough – after the capsize both paddlers would adopt the Screw Roll position with their Canadian blades. The rear man would then bang his paddle twice on the upturned hull as the signal to his partner: one, two, strike!

Setting themselves at the centre of the pool, both men and most of the onlookers drew long deep breaths.

The boat was capsized. Bang, bang, strike!

The whole of the C2 suddenly appeared to lift bodily out of the water, sucking 17 feet by 3 feet of the surface of the pool momentarily after it. It looked like a dog having a pee at both ends on opposite sides, at the same time.

After a brief glimpse of daylight appeared between the deck and the water, the boat crashed down again as both paddlers wrenched themselves free of the cockpits in order to swear at each other – they had forgotten to agree on which side to roll!

Chapter 14 *Steyr Roll*

The Steyr Roll is so named because it was first demonstrated at Steyr in Austria. This roll is also known as the Reverse Pawlata, Lean-back or Back Pawlata.

As with the Pawlata Roll, the extended paddle is swept out to the side prior to the pull-down and Hip Flick, except that in the case of the Steyr Roll the paddle is swept out from the rear.

The Steyr is a very powerful roll, demanding only minimal physical effort from the paddler. The wind-up position is an uncomfortable one, however, and the paddle has to be held in the Extended Paddle Position. For these reasons the roll is not a popular one.

The wind-up

Hold the paddle in the Extended Paddle Position, as if ready to do a Support Stroke on the left side. To get into the wind-up position, lift the paddle across and over on to the right shoulder (*see* fig. 14.1) at the

Fig. 14.1
Placing the paddle in the
wind-up position

Fig. 14.2
Wind-up position A

Fish-eye view

Fig. 14.3
Wind-up position B

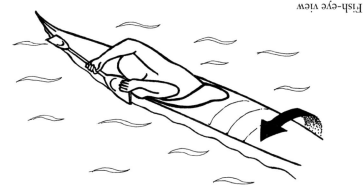

Fish-eye view

same time leaning backwards into one of the positions shown in figures 14.2 and 14.3. Personally, I prefer position A to B. Both positions, however, are equally uncomfortable, especially for the right hand. You will also feel very unstable and you might even capsize, so if you are in a pool, get someone to steady the kayak while you go through your various contortions.

Once in position, you should be lying along the rear deck, although some kayak designs might not allow you to do this. Your trunk should be twisted slightly to the right. The rear blade is angled towards the water. Capsize to the right.

Rolling method

1 Once upside-down, your head should be tilted back, so that you can actually see the stern of the boat.

2 Push your left hand across your face and sweep the paddle outwards (forwards) along the surface (*see* fig. 14.4).

3 At the same time pull downwards. No great effort is needed and you will rise easily to the surface.

Fig. 14.4
Movement diagram:
fish-eye view

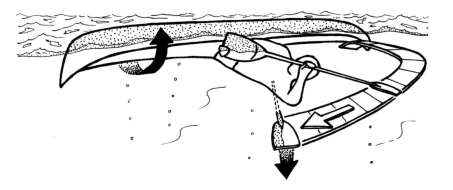

I saw an interesting application of the Steyr Roll some years ago while attending a life-guard demonstration. Two life-guards, paddling kayaks, were demonstrating one of the methods of giving assistance to a supposedly unconscious swimmer in the water. The two paddlers drew up along one side of an inert volunteer, who was floating face down on the surface. Both rescuers were parallel to each other and facing the same way.

The nearest paddler lifted the swimmer's head clear of the water with one hand while placing the swimmer's arms across his deck with the other. The other paddler then took hold of the swimmer's wrists and pulled so that the limp arms were dragged tight across the kayak's deck. The first man leant back into the Steyr Position and capsized inwards towards his partner. As the foredeck turned, it lifted the swimmer partially out of the water. The roll continued and the swimmer was hauled across the two decks and into a position where expired-air resuscitation could be administered.

Care should be taken when attempting the Steyr Roll with kayaks that have equipment on the rear deck. The hood of my paddling jacket once became hooked on the handle of the bilge pump, and it took me what seemed like an age before I realised what had happened – and another age to release it! On another occasion, a tow line on my rear deck had inadvertently become slack enough to hang in a slight loop when the kayak was upside-down. Not knowing this, I managed to hook my paddle into the loop and another little drama ensued.

Alan Byde, *a senior BCU coach, was the first man that I ever saw perform an Eskimo Roll, and it was he who introduced me to the sport of kayaking. Here he tells of a Steyr Roll experience in the Cornish surf.*

In September 1969 I was helping at the annual National Kayak Surfing Championships. There was time off occasionally, and one glorious afternoon – hot sun, big surf – I was enjoying the opportunity of doing some real surfing. By that I mean to run waves which were breaking on average around two metres, long green walls running some distance, before breaking in a steady curl from one end. On the left were some rocks, where the break was best, as there was a sort of compression against them. When running the wave it was better to break towards the right. Left caused problems with big gnarled rocks.

The tide was near the full at spring and rising. I had a slalom kayak of the earliest pointed-nose variety. It was neat and quick to turn. The cockpit was very tight for me, weighing 182 lb, but being snake-hipped I entered easily enough. Exiting was something else. The spray-deck was a very firm fit but it was necessary in big water. It was the sort of kayak that one puts on instead of entering.

Some loops were done – forwards, backwards – and the steady perfect surf rolled in for an hour or two. I was becoming tired and the tide was right up the beach, higher than I had ever seen it before. It was bringing the ever-growing surf closer to suddenly rising sand, where the long break might turn into something a bit dumperish. Deciding that enough was enough, I started to return towards the beach. The break was explosive, the crashing crest blowing out great gouts of spray, as air compressed within the washing machine found a way through the veils of high-power water.

Waiting for the smaller waves to arrive, I made a bad bet and found myself right under the break of a monster. You know when you have done it, for a tiny sigh can be heard just behind the head – a sort of whisper of doom – as the crest starts to slide and tumble just before the wave breaks in earnest. The natural reaction is to glance backwards at more or less shoulder height, then to raise the eyes in disbelief much higher to see the crest overhead. By now the kayak was accelerating like a falling rock, shearing the face of the wave down near the base. Just as the thing breaks the face is momentarily nearly vertical.

Trying vainly to slow things down a bit, I laid right back, head touching the rear deck.

The paddle was gripped firmly ready for a roll from the Steyr (laid-back) position. Overhead, curling brightly against the cerulean blue of the sky the translucent turquoise screen of wave hung shimmering and quivering. It curled a good three feet above the stern. I had time to glance down as I stood on the footbar. The pointed bows were digging into the base of the wave almost at the foot of the face. Add 3 feet to a kayak 13 feet 4 inches long and you have a wave face between 16 and 17 feet high from trough to crest. Then it broke.

The result was an arm-wrenching, body-twisting, head-slamming nastiness. The paddle was ripped free from one hand but the other hand held, at great pain to the wrist, as the long shaft fluttered and swirled in the turmoil inside the wave. It is rightly called the washing machine. There was a rushing and muffled roaring as the huge wave fell into ruin with me lost inside it. Judging by the tumbling sensation I was being rolled over and over inside the break. There was nothing to be done about it except survive.

The rolling ceased after a short while. I wanted air which is usually after seven seconds. I knew I could not breathe. The rolling became a high speed rush, with water searing past my face and arms as I reached out to one side, trying in vain to get my other hand on to the flailing paddle shaft in order to roll. I cannot roll single-handed. My free left hand swung downwards repeatedly, rather as a swimmer might strike to raise the head, and indeed my head rose slightly to the surface. The dark green turned to white as my face was bathed in froth.

I managed to get a gasp of air and water mixed, which made me want to cough. That is bad practice under water because the next human reaction is to gasp in air, and air I did not have. Again I fumbled for the paddle shaft and several times my fingers touched it but it was whirled away again before I could close my grasp.

By this time I had been going less than a minute, but not much less. I was wracked with a desire to cough but I knew I must not. Mind took charge over matter.

The surface water was surging forwards over the lower layer of water, the broken surface called the 'soup' by surfers. The left hand was reaching down again, striking to rotate the body towards the surface to get another gasp of air. This was successful and set me up a little longer. A moment later I could grab the thrashing paddle shaft, as the rush was easing a little. Taking hold, resisting the desire to attempt a roll, knowing that I might have the wrong angle on the blade, setting the paddle for a roll, I waited. Intense self-control was necessary and it came to me. Taking care with my preparation I rolled up first time. The chance to breathe again was a joyful thing. We take it all for granted usually. The sun seemed beautiful, the warmth of the air a contrast to the rushing chill of the seawater. A voice shouted in my ear; a fellow paddler who had been sitting on the cliffs with some others had seen me go under the monster break. They had all shouted with surprise and alarm for me, but that is the way it goes. They had continued to sit and to watch, and I was gone from view a long time, some say half a minute. Then the upturned hull was seen tearing in on the soup, but no sign of a roll.

It was then that my 'rescuer' had become alarmed, and had scrambled down the low cliffs and run down the short beach and struggled out into the raging thrash of the broken waves to arrive beside me as I in fact rolled. He was angry with me. He thought I was showing off, with a delayed roll!

There is a sweetness in being able to breathe

again. The experience I had is something rare which I am pleased to recall, but never want to go through again. Some may enquire why I did not bale out? It did not occur to me, but I felt I stood a better chance by staying in the tight cockpit and persevering. The knowledge of life, the experience of living, is intensified by many degrees by such a life-threatening risk. In order to live a little, one must die a little. Some fail to make it to safety.

The author surfaces while practising a Steyr Roll in a swimming pool. Added leverage from the extended paddle, coupled with the lean-back body position give this roll tremendous power. The plume of water shows the direction taken by the head as it lifts during the last stage of the roll. To perform a comfortable Steyr Roll, you need a kayak with a flat or low rear deck so when you lean well back you can touch the deck with the back of your head during the wind-up. In this picture the author is using a white-water kayak. Photo courtesy Derek C. Hutchinson

CHAPTER 15 *Eskimo Storm Roll*

This roll (*see* fig. 15.1) was used by the Eskimos of the Angmagssalik area of East Greenland. Their kayaks tended to be about 19 to 20 feet long with a beam of 20 inches and a depth of between 6 and 7 inches. The more sheer (i.e. curve of the deck up to the bow and the stern) the kayak, the easier it should be to roll, since the 'banana' shape will encourage the inverted kayak to turn on to its side and so help the action of the roll. The decks of the Angmagssalik kayaks were flat and so perhaps not as easy to roll as those kayaks from the west coast of Greenland.

Fig. 15.1
Movement diagram:
fish-eye view

The wind-up

The wind-up is the same as for the Pawlata Roll, except that there is no need to concentrate on the planing angle of the extended paddle blade.

Rolling method

1 Once upside-down, move the forward paddle blade out to an angle of 30° from the side of the kayak.

2 Lean well forwards and push upwards with the right hand until the forward paddle blade is about a foot above the surface.

3 Now pull down violently so that the raised blade slaps the water. You will rise to the surface very quickly. The blade strikes the surface, then planes out sideways as the roll nears completion.

The first time I tried this, I had no idea just how powerful this roll was. I came to the surface with such force that, in my surprise, I threw myself over into another capsize.

Paul Hoobyar *is a well-known paddler now living in Seattle. He recounts the following memorable occasion.*

This epic run took place in the month of January – a time in these parts when daylight is rarely given a chance to flourish.

The river was high from incessant rains, and we all thought it a grand idea to paddle the neighbourhood Class II run with the water so high. Our friendly Rouge River took on a character more akin to its name, for logs and debris were catapulted downstream in the frothy, brown waters.

Currents snapped and billowed as we stood with our kayaks in hand at the bank, gazing at the scene before us. Eddylines had turned into beach-heads of confused, undulating seascapes. Boils rose up angrily from out of the maelstrom. Rapids that normally existed on this run were drowned, covered by thousands of cubic feet of rain-fed flooding. Other places which were normally placid at summer flows were agitated with the mad foamings of a flood falling over itself. Our familiar little kayak-run seethed and tore at anything in reach.

Timidly we made our way downstream, vaulting over the explosive heights of enormous standing waves, catching glimpses of what lay downstream while perched atop these watery mountains. Fearful of falling into any abyss, we tried to keep our eyes void of grit and water.

At one bend in the river, a dyke of bedrock extended out into the current. Normally this rock sits high above the water level, looking down on the river as it flows past. But today that dyke angled the river. Its terminus was buried deep below the raging currents and water billowed over it. A boiling, churning eddy was created behind this rock pier. One of the more foolhardy (or courageous) in our group paddled out of the eddy, pointing the nose of his kayak at the cascade of water falling over the dyke and charging ahead. He was catapulted like a watermelon seed pinched between two huge fingers into the air.

The entire three metres of his kayak sailed high above the surface of the water before he began his descent back to the swirling brown water.

Having seen one in our group survive, we all made sport of the place. After a couple of rocket rides and end-over-ends, I dropped the nose of my kayak into a different spot behind the weir where the bedrock was closer to the surface. The nose of my kayak was forced down by the oncoming current and hit the bedrock below like the blade of a guillotine slamming home to the block.

For a second, my feet and knees felt trapped, pinched by the collapse of deck and hull around them, but shortly the plastic kayak regained its shape. I was slammed upside-down like I had paddled into a large tumble-drier. While I struggled to get my paddle to the surface, and not have it ripped out of my hands by the currents yanking and slamming on my body, my whole lower body was chilled by river water.

'Damn! My spray-skirt popped', I thought to myself. 'Better make this roll count and quickly.'

When I had my paddle on the surface, and felt my body in the proper position, I swept out and back hard with my upper body. I wanted up!

I was resurrected from the cold inky world of the river (love those Eskimos) only to realise that my kayak was sinking! Two feet of the nose of my old tupperware boat had broken clean off by the impact with the rock, and as I looked down in terror at my paddling partners over in the eddy, they broke down in a fit of belly-laughing at my sinking predicament. Friends? . . . huh!

Could this be called a Vertical Screw Roll? This 'surprise' roll was captured during a game of polo. Caught unaware while paddling backwards too fast, the author pulls back on his right hand to bring the short kayak upright. PHOTO COURTESY DEREK C. HUTCHINSON

Chapter 16 *Vertical Storm Roll*

This is a deep roll which was used in rough, foaming conditions. Its aim was to take support from the solid green water well below the surface.

The wind-up

The wind-up position is the same as for the Storm Roll. Hold the paddle as shown in figure 16.1.

Fig. 16.1
Movement diagram:
fish-eye view

Rolling method

1 Once you are upside-down, move the paddle out to an angle of 30° from the hull of the kayak.

2   The extended blade is held in a vertical position when it is pushed above the surface of the water. The edge of the blade nearest the water is angled slightly outwards from the kayak.

3   When the downward strike is made, the angle of the blade begins to plane slightly and by the time it is two to three feet below the surface of the water, it is planing well outwards. In this position, the blade is able to give support for the downward pull.

Liz Sharman, *Ladies' World Slalom Champion, has been European Champion twice and National Champion nine times. Out of a wealth of experience she chose to tell the following:*

I was paddling at Tacen in Yugoslavia a few years ago, competing in the Europa Cup. At the start of the course there is a huge man-made weir that has a sluice gate at the top. The sluice gate isn't very high, then everything just drops away suddenly. It's like being on a giant roller-coaster at a fairground. The water banks up on one side, rolls down, then banks up on the other, then banks up yet again on the other side before dropping into this huge hole at the bottom. A lot of people have had accidents on this part of the course. C1 paddlers especially, have been getting their noses wiped away, because this chute has a very rough concrete bottom – everybody is quite nervous of it. Well, they'd positioned two gates in this awful place, and naturally, you don't have a cat-in-hell's chance of even seeing them because you're going so fast.

When it was my turn, I shot off the start line and sprinted the hundred or so yards to the sluice. Unfortunately I hit my paddle on the top of the sluice gate and promptly capsized. So there I was, going down this deep, zoom-foam type horrific white-water scenario, thinking, 'Where on earth am I?' I just hung on and waited for everything to stop boiling and pushing me around and then I rolled up. Of all things, I rolled up straight in line with the gate which I went through to carry on and finish the course. That was the run that won me the slalom.

My nastiest rolling experience was at Bala Mill Fall on the Tryweryn. Somehow, I managed to capsize at the top and dropped down several stages of the fall on my head. When I finally got to the bottom, I thought I'd pull myself together and wait for all the turbulence and pushing around to stop. When I finally rolled up, I found that my crash helmet had split in two and it was hanging in two halves – one half around each ear.

It's interesting, because I learned to roll a kayak before I could paddle one in a straight line. So rolling was taught to me as a basic stroke. Right from the first, I was competent at keeping the correct way up or getting back up the right way before I ever went out on to an open river. That gave me a great deal of confidence, which helped me proceed very quickly through the slalom divisions.

CHAPTER 17 *Greenland Roll*

The wind-up

The kayaker holds the paddle as shown against the gunwale with the blade at right angles to the water (*see* fig. 17.1). The man leans forward and slightly towards the paddle. The palms of both hands are touching the outside face of the paddle blade so that the knuckles face outwards.

Rolling method

1 Once upside-down, the paddler pushes both hands upwards. At the same time, the wrists are flicked outwards, parallel to the surface of the water. The paddle is now in the planing angle for the outward sweep (*see* fig. 17.1).

Fig. 17.1
Movement diagram:
fish-eye view

Fig. 17.2
Final brace with forward
scull

2 By pivoting from the waist and hips, the paddler sweeps the extended paddle out in an arc from the side of the kayak. At the end of the sweep, when the blade reaches a position at right angles to the boat, the palms of the paddler will face upwards (*see* fig. 17.2).

3 The left hand has been the pivot point of the sweep and it is now the fulcrum for the support stroke. The paddler pulls violently downwards on the paddle for the final lift. If necessary, the lift can be completed by a forward sculling movement prior to the brace.

Greenland Kingumut Naatillugu (Forward Sweeping Roll)

For normal kayaking in stormy weather or for rolling practice, the Greenland hunter is completely sealed from the effects of cold water by his tuilik or full kayak jacket. In warm weather or for recreational contests, the paddler may wear a garment known as a tuitok or spray apron. In many ways this is similar to our modern spray-skirt, but instead of using shock cord, the tuitok is fastened around the cockpit rim by means of a draw cord. The top of the tube fits loosely over the chest under the armpits of the paddler and is held in place by two shoulder straps. If the paddler has to roll, a certain amount of water will

Fig. 17.3
Greenland
Kingumut
Naatillugu

naturally find its way into the kayak through the top opening. The Forward Sweeping Roll is often used because it reduces the amount of water scooped up by the top edge of the tuitok as the paddler rolls to the surface.

THE WIND-UP
The wind-up or surface preparatory position is shown in figure 17.3 for a roll in a clockwise direction. Holding the paddle in the extended position with the palms facing outwards, the paddler twists the upper part of his body round to the left. The extended blade is hooked over the starboard gunwale. In order to capsize over the starboard side, the left knee is lifted up and the head is thrown backwards.

ROLLING METHOD
To start with, the paddler's body is almost lying backwards on the rear deck. He unwinds by performing a Reverse Sweep towards the bow, pushing his body forwards and keeping the leading edge of the paddle at a planing angle. The paddler rolls up, leaning over the fore-deck. The dotted lines in figure 17.3 illustrate the underwater view of the roll.

Chris Hare, *a BCU senior coach, was a member of the British Geological and Kayaking Expedition to Ubekendt Ejeland, West Greenland, in 1966. He describes one of the glorious days he spent with the villagers of Igdlorssuit.*

Igdlorssuit (latitude 74° North longtitude 55° West), on the West Coast of Greenland, is a tiny bay on a forgotten island, with a population of about 100 people. Today, however, was a great day. The population had doubled with an influx of hunters and families from Umanak. They spilled out of the tiny wooden shacks on to the green volcanic sand of the bay to watch the kayak hunters show off their skills.

After a number of kayak races the word got round that 'qajassuaq' – that was what they called me – was good at rolling. Now I wanted to learn some rolling methods from them, but in order to do that, I had to get out there and do some myself. I hoped that seeing me as a challenge might overcome some of their inhibitions. The fact that I could roll, I suppose, made me unique in that I was a European in Greenland who could roll. Let's face it: I think they thought that only Greenlanders could live in a kayak.

Be that as it may, this chap came along, built like a typical Inuit – short, stocky and very powerful. He and I got on the water and set to work rolling. I forget now how we communicated, but it was decided that we should do a different roll each time. To my amazement I beat him. It was not really my intention to beat anyone there, in fact just the reverse. As far as I remember I did the Pawlata, the Screw, the Steyr (always my favourite) and the Put-Across, and as many variations as I could think of. The opposition kept coming up with variations on a Screw that I could not imagine being possible, so I finished up with the 'hats off' trick (the one where you roll without getting your hat wet). I remember the trick nearly went wrong. I was using a kayak belonging to one of the villagers and for some reason – it might have been that the hull was a different shape from that which I was used to – when I was upside-down, I couldn't get my hands across the upturned hull to pass the hat over.

I did some quick thinking: death before dishonour, the people of Igdlorssuit were all watching me uphold the prestige of 'our' village. (I think if I had left the boat I would have been an outcast.) What I did was to put the hat over as far as I could. Then I sort of swam underneath to the other side, put my hand up, grabbed the hat and rolled up, putting on the still dry hat. The villagers cheered and I think they all got drunk after that – I tried, but the beer was too weak!

CHAPTER 18 *Earliest rolling methods*

The following account by David Crantz of the earliest-known recorded methods of the Eskimo Roll will be a challenge to anyone who feels that all the known methods have been mastered.

'1 The Greenlander lays himself first on one side, then on the other, with his body flat upon the water (to imitate the case of one who is nearly, but not quite overset) and keeps the balance with his pautik or oar, so that he raises himself again.

2 He overturns himself quite, so that his head hangs perpendicular underwater; in this dreadful posture he gives himself a swing with a stroke of his paddle, and raises himself aloft again on which side he will.

These are the most common cases of misfortune, which frequently occur in storms and high waves; but they still suppose that the Greenlander retains the advantage of his pautik in his hand, and is disentangled from the seal-leather strap. But it may easily happen in the seal-fishery that the man becomes entangled with the string, so that he cannot rightly use the pautik, or that he loses it entirely. Therefore they must be prepared for this casualty. With this view:

3 They run one end of the pautik under one of the cross strings of the kayak (to imitate its being entangled), overset, and scramble up again by means of the artful motion of the other end of the pautik.

4 They hold one end of it in their mouth, and yet move the other end with their hand, so as to rear themselves upright again.

5 They lay the pautik behind their neck, and hold it there with both hands or,

6 Hold it fast behind their back; so overturn, and by stirring it with both their hands behind them, without bringing it before, rise and recover.

7 They lay it across one shoulder, take hold of it with one hand before, and the other behind their back, and thus emerge from the deep.

The sight of native hunters rolling completely round and up to the surface again in their kayaks mystified and thrilled the early visitors and explorers to Greenland – witness the text which accompanies this delightful illustration of an 'Eskimo Feat – A Summerset':

'About this time I enjoyed a rare sight. One of the Esquimaux turned summersets in the water seated in his kyack! [sic] Over and over his kyack went, till we cried "Enough!" and yet he wet only his hands and face! This is a feat performed only by a few. It requires great skill and strength to do it. One miss in the stroke of the oar as they pass from the centre (when their head and body are underwater) to the surface might terminate fatally. No one will attempt this feat, however, unless a companion in his kyak is near.'

FROM *Life with the Esquimaux* BY CAPTAIN CHARLES FRANCIS HALL, VOL. I, pp. 73–4,
SAMPSON LOW, SON & MARSTON, 1864

These exercises are of service in cases where the pautik is entangled with the string; but because they may also quite lose it, in which the greatest danger lies, therefore,

8 Another exercise is to run the pautik through the water under the kayak, hold it fast on both sides with their face laying on the kayak, in this position overturn, and rise again by moving the oar *secundum artem* on the top of the water from beneath. This is of service when they lose the oar during the oversetting, and yet see it swimming over them, to learn to manage it with both hands from below.

9 They let the oar go, turn themselves head down, reach their hands after it, and from the surface pull it down to them, and so rebound up.

10 But if they cannot possibly reach it, they take either the hand-board off the harpoon, or a knife, and try by the force of these, even splashing the water with the palm of their hand to swing themselves above the water; but this seldom succeeds.'

DAVID CRANTZ, History of Greenland, 1767

Barry Howell, *an experienced white-water and sea paddler, recalls an early assessment day in Cornwall.*

Some years ago, and early in my sea-canoeing 'career', I decided to throw caution to the winds and present myself for assessment for the sea kayak proficiency award. Secure in the knowledge that there was undoubtedly safety in numbers, a mate of mine that I'd paddled with for a few years came along too. We assembled on the Friday night at Penzance YMCA, as the course was organised and run by the Cornwall Canoe Association.

We looked a motley crew, with blatantly obvious differences in experience, but the introductory session passed reasonably well, without too many errors on my part. It was an obvious error to find myself locked out of the YMCA after closing time – and an even worse mistake to choose the chief examiner's room to break into – but that's another story.

It puzzled us that there was one member of the course who hadn't said a word so far. Even when asked a direct question, he just looked demoniacally at the questioner, and made strange noises in his throat. The examiner

didn't seem to mind this, and acted as if it were commonplace.

During the Saturday, while we were going through our paces out in St Michael's Bay, it transpired that the paddler in question had a chronic stutter, and just dried up completely in moments of excitement. Struggling silences of a minute or so, while he attempted to get the words out were not uncommon, but we soon got used to protracted conversation.

The Sunday dawned brilliantly, with the kind of monstrous swell that only Cornwall can produce. Assembled on the beach at Sennen, we looked out in horror at the surf coming in from what seemed like miles out. Our patient examiner looked blithely at the team. 'No problem', he said, 'make your own way out beyond the break line and then we'll get together as a group again.' With that, he jumped into his boat and paddled off, leaving us looking at each other, somewhat sheepishly.

Well, it was an assessment situation, so we felt that we ought to give it a go. Summoning unknown courage, and dripping adrenalin, the team set off to follow the examiner, paddling line abreast out into the surf. If you have ever paddled out through big surf, you will know the feeling. You almost start to believe that you have the situation under control, when the wave of the day appears on the horizon, and you know beyond all doubt that it's guaranteed to break on you just as you reach it.

Paddling frantically, the team sprinted for the oncoming wall of water in an attempt to climb up and over it before it reached the critical point. It was going to be touch and go. Roughly half of us made it to the top, the other half got 'creamed'. There sat the examiner on the seaward side, smiling contentedly as the survivors paddled up to him.

'I suppose we'd better surf back in and see what has happened to the others', he said, and paddled off to catch the next wave. We followed and assembled once again on the beach, recounting tales of the horrors of Cornish surf. All except one paddler. There was no sign of the man with the stutter. We looked around in dismay, until one of the group shouted and pointed out towards the water. There, up to his chest in the waves, was the missing paddler – looking very sorry for himself. He dragged himself towards us, towing the two halves of his boat behind him, and with the cockpit coaming hung around his neck. We dashed down to help him in. The examiner strode up, a sympathetic look in his eye. 'Everything all right?' he asked. Back came the reply as quick as a flash: ' . . . sh . . . sh . . . sh . . . sh**!'

Chapter 19 *Kotzebue Roll*

The kayak

The kayaks from Kotzebue Sound were long, fast, slender craft with only a small amount of freeboard. They were from 17 to 18 feet long, and 17 to 18 inches wide. Normally a double-bladed paddle would be used for hunting, but a single-bladed paddle, carried conveniently in the fore-deck straps would be used for rolling.

The wind-up

Let us assume that the kayaker is paddling with the single blade on his left side. The palm of the right hand holding the T-bar will be facing downwards. To adopt the wind-up position, the paddle would be lifted over to the right side but without changing the position of the hands on the shaft. Using the right hand as a fulcrum, the T-bar would be allowed to rotate in the palm as the paddle moves across in an arc overhead, to a position on the paddler's right side. The paddle is now in a vertical position, the blade facing the gunwale. The palm of the right hand will now be facing upwards, with the fingers curled around the T-bar and straddling the shaft.

Rolling method

1 The paddler capsizes to the right. The paddle remains vertical. The right hand pushes towards the surface and acts as the fulcrum.

2 The left elbow moves forward as the left hand rotates round the shaft until the knuckles face towards the stern.

3 The left hand pulls the paddle downwards. In so doing the left bicep should brush across the nose at the same time as the kayak rises to the surface.

Fig. 19.1
Movement diagram

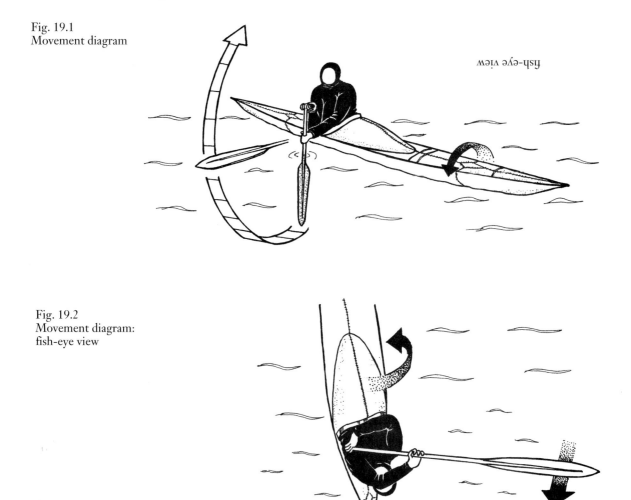

fish-eye view

Fig. 19.2
Movement diagram:
fish-eye view

As an alternative to pushing the right hand towards the surface, the T-bar can be drawn in across the body (*see* fig. 19.2). The paddler leans back and, still using the right hand as the fulcrum, strikes down with the extended paddle.

CHAPTER 20 *Nunivak Island Roll*

The kayak

The Nunivak Island kayak (*see* fig. 20.1) was held in high regard by all those who were familiar with it and it was generally considered one of the most seaworthy of all the Alaskan kayaks. In a manner similar to other Bering Sea kayaks, it was propelled by a single-bladed paddle. The boat was short by Arctic standards, the longest of this type being no more than 15 feet 9 inches. It was also very beamy with a width of 32 inches.

Fig. 20.1
Kayak (qayaq) and paddle (anguarun) from Nunivak Island

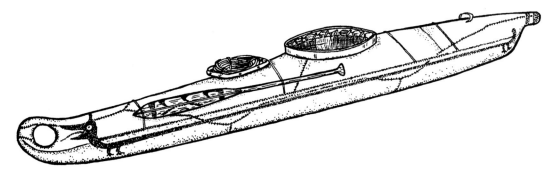

These kayaks were good load-carrying boats so, as would be expected, they were of considerable volume, being approximately 16 inches deep in the vicinity of the cockpit. This manhole was very large, with room to carry a passenger back-to-back with the paddler, if necessary. The circumference of the opening was over eight feet. During a roll this would be a very large hole to make watertight. To achieve this the paddler wore a knee-length kayak jacket which was flared at the bottom so that it could fit around and be laced to the rim of the manhole. In the event of a capsize, the voluminous garment would allow the kayaker to wriggle down inside the kayak, while the jacket still retained its seal around the coaming, and to perform a roll. Once on the surface the paddler would have to pull out the folds of the jacket so that any water that had been collected there could be dumped out.

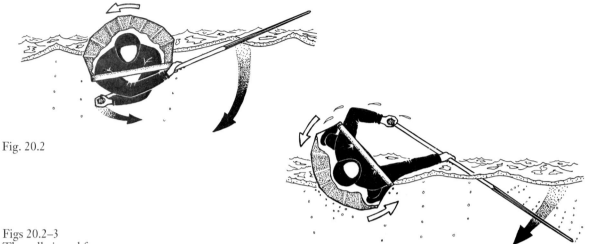

Fig. 20.2

Figs 20.2–3
The roll viewed from
the rear

Fig. 20.3

Rolling method

1 Once withdrawn inside the hull (*see* figs 20.2 and 20.3), the paddler would have to wedge himself tightly as best he could, with his legs apart, gripping the sides, or with his knees drawn up and his legs jammed between the deck and the bottom of the hull. The Nunivak kayak did not have any longitudinal lathes running alongside the main deck support, under which a man could brace his knees.

2 The fingers of the inboard hand curled under the T-bar handle, with the thumb towards the kayak. The shaft would usually part the index and middle fingers. The palm of the outboard hand faced away from the paddler.

3 Once the kayaker was in position, the paddle was swept downwards in a manner similar to the modern Put-Across Roll. If necessary the roll could be finished by a scull.

The fore- and aft decks of the Nunivak kayaks were steeply pitched. This quality would assist the turning action of the kayak during the roll.

It is possible to practise this roll in a modern kayak. You are certainly not going to be able to wriggle inside your modern fibreglass sea boat, but if it has a flat rear deck, it will be possible to lean back along it and practise rolling up with the paddle held in the Nunivak position.

CHAPTER 2I *King Island Roll*

The kayak

The overall shape of the King Island kayak is similar to that of the Nunivak Island kayak. The King Island boat, however, is a scaled-down version of the latter, being only 25 inches wide and 15 feet long. Like the Nunivak Island kayak it is a large-volume boat, with a depth of approximately 16 inches in the region of the cockpit.

The wind-up

Fig. 21.1
Movement diagram:
fish-eye view

To wind-up, the paddle is held level with the chest and at right angles to the kayak. The blade is parallel to the surface of the water. The paddler capsizes (*see* fig. 21.1). It makes no difference whether the arms are extended during the capsize or when the body comes to rest in the fully inverted position.

Rolling method

1 Once upside-down, the paddle should still be at right angles to the kayak. The T-bar is rotated slightly forward so that the leading edge of the blade is angled at about 10°–15° to the surface of the water.

2 To bring the paddle to the surface for the roll up, the kayaker sweeps the paddle in the direction indicated by the ribbon arrow. The paddle angle will cause it to rise to the surface and give support to the final downward pull by the paddler.

It is possible to practise this roll in a modern kayak using a double-bladed paddle. However, I have always found that this particular roll demands considerable effort.

A lone paddler rolling in the cold North Sea near the Longstone lighthouse. The first time you roll in really cold water, the effect on your unprotected temples can be quite stunning. You'll find it pays to wear a neoprene helmet if you intend to practise your rolls in cold water. PHOTO: DEREK C. HUTCHINSON

John Heath, *from Damon, Texas, has been a 'student' of the Eskimo Roll in all its forms since the 1950s. I personally consider him to be one of the world's foremost authorities on this particular branch of Eskimo culture. What follows is part of an article, 'Alaskan Eskimo Rolls' which first appeared in the 1986 Winter edition of* Sea Kayaker *magazine.*

Throughout the ten years that I lived in Seattle, my neighbours went out of their way to be friendly. Except one. This middle-aged widow had been friendly enough at first, but then she stopped speaking to me. It finally got to the point where she would even cross the street to avoid passing me on the sidewalk.

As I looked towards her house one day,

wondering what might be the source of the problem, I realised that she was the only neighbour who could see into my living room. Not that she would peep, but the drapes were usually left open to the lake and mountain view, and as I recalled some of the things that took place near that window, I could understand how anyone might want to take a second look if they happened to glance in that direction at certain times.

That part of my living room was the area in which numerous armchair Eskimo rolling sessions had taken place. My guests and I had stood or sat on the floor near that window and used brooms or dust-mops as paddles to explain or learn the mechanics of a certain roll. By using brooms or dust-mops as paddles, we reduced the chances of injury to furniture or humans if we should get carried away in our demonstrations. It helped to learn the basics of a roll before practising it in a swimming pool, not only for convenience, but to save money in pool rental time.

So it was that my guests and I stood and leaned backward or bent forward while simulating roll movements, or rolled on the floor and swept a broom across the carpet. We didn't stop to think that, to a non-kayaker, we might look like drunks trying to clean the room.

However, if the armchair rolling sessions were the cause of my being a social outcast, it was pointless to pursue the matter. It would only have made things worse if I mentioned it and my neighbour HADN'T seen me waving a broom.

Among my guests in Seattle during the 1960s were a dozen or so Alaskan Eskimos. Most of them were from the last generation of their region to have made and used kayaks, and two of them could roll. So the rolls they described to me were taught to me at home, using the broom and dust-mop method, then practised later in a kayak.

Alaskan Eskimo Rolls are an interesting contrast to those of Greenland. Single-bladed paddles were used even in Kotzebue Sound, where the double-bladed paddle was preferred for ordinary paddling. In fact, my informants thought it would be impossible to roll with a double-bladed paddle, which shows how easy it is to become locked in a certain way of thinking. It appears that if rolling with a double-bladed paddle was ever known in Alaska, it probably would have been in the Aleutian Islands. Unfortunately, the skill of the Aleut kayakers was declining before cameras came into use, so much of their paddling technique has been lost forever.

Rolling seems never to have been as important in Alaska as it was in Greenland, where it is still taught today. This was because of a difference in the hunting techniques used, and a difference in the way in which equipment had evolved. Greenlanders sometimes kayaked near huge glaciers, which could calve icebergs suddenly, creating giant waves that would capsize any kayak. On the other hand, Alaskan kayakers had some warning if a storm approached. They could head homeward or, if that became impractical, they could raft up and ride out the storm. The projectiles thrown at seals and other quarry from kayaks in Alaska were more often of the self-contained dart variety, i.e. they were free of the kayak once they had been thrown and were unlikely to cause a capsize. Greenlanders relied heavily on the use of harpoons with a line and float, which was efficient but required split-second timing to avoid becoming entangled and being capsized.

Since rolling wasn't as important in Alaska,

it does not appear that many methods were ever developed, and the percentage of kayakers who knew how to roll was probably always lower in Alaska than it was in Greenland, where at least thirty methods were known. The variations and combinations of Greenland rolls are so numerous that different observers might see a given roll as a method or as a variation on another method, so it is a moot point as to the total number known.

King Island informants told me of a rescue method that involved crawling up inside the kayak and awaiting rescue. If they were wearing a kayak jacket, which was fastened around their face, wrists, and cockpit rim, they could grab the topknot of the hood, which was for that purpose, and pull it down over their face so that their head was in the hull, but their arms were still in the sleeves. There was enough air in the hull to sustain them if help was nearby. This was preferable to bailing out into almost freezing water. But if help didn't arrive, it would have been possible to reach a spare paddle on the fore-deck and, using a variation of the Put-Across Roll, to roll up while still in the hull, with only the paddle and hands above the cockpit rim. None of my informants had ever heard of such an incident, but I have experimented with the method in a replica kayak and it can be done.

One of my guests in Seattle in 1966 was Chester Seveck, who had spent many years as a government reindeer herder in the Kotzebue Sound area where he had also worked as a tour guide. Thus he had become a sort of professional Eskimo, whose job was to meet airline flights at the Kotzebue airport and explain the local lifestyle to tour groups.

At first I was sceptical of getting kayak data from a herder-cum-tour guide. But I was wrong in prejudging Chester. Not only was he knowledgeable and articulate, but his experience with tourists' questions had honed his communicative skills to the point that he was one of the best informants I have ever known.

The usual pattern of kayak used in Kotzebue Sound was about 17 or 18 feet long with a beam of 18 to 20 inches. It had a low profile and a slight reverse sheer that levelled towards the ends. The bow had a slight upturn. The fore-deck was raised forward of the small cockpit in order to provide legroom and shed water that might fall on the occupant. The cockpit rim was raked, which facilitated entry and exit, and provided elbow clearance when using the double-bladed paddle.

A longitudinally attached strip of antler or bone was pegged to the deck ridge just forward of the cockpit. This prevented paddle wear on the skin cover, and since it was about the level of the kayaker's lower chest, served as a paddle-rest when using the double-bladed paddle. The paddle was not lifted off in normal cruising. The raised fore-deck was cosy when paddling against a cold wind. I recall a day at Kotzebue in 1970 when it was almost freezing and I was paddling against a breeze that came off the sea ice, but the raised fore-deck gave good protection from the cold.

From 1966 to 1971, several King Island Eskimos were frequent visitors to Seattle and I visited them in Alaska in 1970. In those days, two King Islanders were left who knew how to roll. One of these, Leo Kunnuk, taught me how to do it at home by standing in front of me, using the mop, while I followed his every move standing behind him with my broom. The King Island Roll is three-dimensional and complicated, so if my neighbour saw us repeating it over and over, I wouldn't have blamed her for calling some friends over and serving refreshments, because it WOULD have been hilarious to watch.

CHAPTER 22 *Put-Across Roll*

I remember a time when the Put-Across Roll was very popular with kayak instructors. This was because it was a very uncomplicated manoeuvre and therefore easy to teach. Unfortunately, simplicity is its only charm.

There is no wind-up position for the Put-Across Roll. To get ready for the roll, the kayaker has to place the paddle on the surface of the water, using only one hand, which holds the paddle precariously by the tip. Any swirl or eddy, even a slight gust of wind, can cause him to part company with his only means of propulsion. This is a pity because, most often, capsizes occur in poor conditions. Getting into position can hardly be done quickly, and a kayaker might easily be swept into danger or hit by the next wave whilst preparing himself.

Rolling method

1 Once you have capsized, the paddle is passed across the body to the side upon which the roll is to be performed. Reach up to the surface and place the paddle so that it floats at right angles to the kayak (*see* fig. 22.1). (If on moving water, this is the time when you may have to say goodbye to your paddle.)

2 Now, with the hand that placed the paddle on the surface, take hold of the nearest corner of the blade, as if for a Support Stroke. Reach up to the surface with the other hand (*see* fig. 22.2) and take hold of the shaft.

3 Now pull down smartly. This violent pull, combined with a Hip Flick, should bring you to the surface (*see* fig. 22.3).

The Put-Across Roll has no real application in modern kayaking. However, it is ideal to use as a follow-up exercise to the Support Stroke or Brace (*see* p. 27).

I do not recommend the Put-Across Roll as a remedy for any accidental capsize.

Stages of the roll

Fig. 22.1
Positioning the paddle:
fish-eye view

Fig. 22.2
Reaching towards the
surface: fish-eye view

Fig. 22.3
The pull-down and Hip
Flick: fish-eye view

Paul Caffyn *is a well-known New Zealand ocean kayak paddler. Among his exploits is a 1,500-mile first circumnavigation of the North Island of New Zealand which he completed in 75 days in his kayak 'Isadora'. These extracts are taken from his book* Obscured by Waves *(pp. 81 and 164), which tells the story of his trip.*

Slowly we nosed towards the beach, with our eyes frequently searching over our shoulders for the waves coming through. A large wave appeared. It picked up *Isadora* and I hung in a right rudder as we sped down the face of the wave. Max was about 20 yards away to my right when the wave picked us up. Unfortunately he'd taken off on the same wave and hung in a left rudder as he careered down the face of the wave.

Both of us thought we were home and hosed. Then came the horrifying realisation that we were racing towards each other on collision course. There was no time to take evasive action. I was a little higher up the face of the wave than Max and shot over the deck of his canoe, just in front of the cockpit. I flicked the paddle up to miss his head and Max had to arch his body over backwards so that my skeg didn't cut him.

Next moment I was upside-down and gasping for air in the aftermath of the wave. The paddle was gone and the force of the water had pushed the spray-skirt partially off. Max backpaddled to me and I was using the stern of his canoe to roll back up when the next wave struck. Max had to go with it. Short of air inside this wave, I came out of the cockpit and in the wake of it retrieved the paddle. I was swimming shorewards towing *Isadora* by her bow when Max attempted to tow me in. Yet another large wave tore my grip from his decklines. This wave flipped Max stern over bow in a forward loop. For a fraction of a second, I glimpsed the yellow hull of his canoe standing on end, contrasted against the black of the night sky.

Max attempted to roll but gave up after a struggle in the broken waves. He slipped out of his cockpit and joined me in the water. In the dark, we towed our capsized canoes shore-wards, the broken waves helping to push us in until at last my wet-suit bootie touched a rock. We could walk in the rest of the way, but we still had 150 yards to go before collapsing in a heap amongst the large boulders of the beach, exhausted, but thankful to be there in one piece with the boats intact.

'If only you hadn't hooked left', I groaned.
'If only you hadn't hooked right', Max replied.

As I headed into the gap, the swell was no more than four feet from crest to trough. I was half-way through and had just paddled over one crest; then I saw the following swell crest, a wall of water that reared up six or seven feet in height. In the narrow gap, the water level dropped rapidly like someone had pulled out the plug. Both against the small rock and the wall of the sea stack, the face of this huge swell started to break. A fraction of a second later, the bow disappeared in the V of the surging wall of water. Then I was completely buried by the broken wave with no support for the paddle in the aerated water. With the horrifying realisation that, 'this is it, the finish', *Isadora* and I were upside-down.

A second, large freak swell broke even before my head surfaced after the first one. My greatest fear was being smashed up against the rocky walls. At last the white foam disappeared and I was able to gasp a lungful of air. With the paddle on one side of the capsized hull and my head on the other I decided not to attempt to roll but to push *Isadora* out of the gap. With the speed that only comes from staring death in the face, I was out of the cockpit, had shoved *Isadora* hard to the south, and retrieved the paddle. On the south side of the sea stacks, yet another worry flashed through my mind – the two knot north-east-going current would push the canoe back on to the rocks.

It took me a while to catch up with the drifting canoe and even longer to get back into the cockpit. Four times, I managed to sit astride the cockpit only to roll over gracefully as I tried to slide my legs in. The chilling cold of the sea was starting to numb my fingers – time for extreme measures. I pulled the closed cell foam mat out from its position on the floor of the cockpit, placed it on the surface of the sea, and laid the paddle blade on top. Using this as a primitive form of outrigger, it was easy to slide my legs into the cockpit. Still retaining the support of the buoyant mat, I worked the bilge pump handle to empty out the cockpit until my right arm was tired. Then I bailed with a wet-suit bootie which had slipped off in the fracas.

The cockpit was now dry but I was still shaking from fright and the cold and it was a struggle to move the back-rest into position. I put the spray-skirt back on then pulled on the light plastic gloves and parka to staunch the numbing cold. After a quick glance up to the distant light-tower, I paddled cautiously away to the south-west, in an attempt to stop the cold.

Chapter 23   *The Headstand*

The Headstand was first publicised in Germany more than forty years ago as part of some rolling instructions. Strictly speaking it is not really a roll, but more a Support Stroke, i.e. you go over and come up on the same side.

Method

1 Figure 23.1 shows how to capsize on the right-hand side. As you capsize, allow the right blade to slice down, bringing the left one over.

Stages of the roll (continued over page)

Fig. 23.1
Paddle movement for the capsize

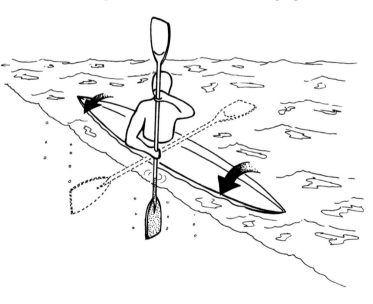

2 While this is happening, change your hand position. Let go of the shaft with your left hand and grasp the lower blade, fingers outward. Turn your right hand over on the paddle shaft so that your palm is facing outward (*see* fig. 23.2).

**Stages of the roll,
continued**

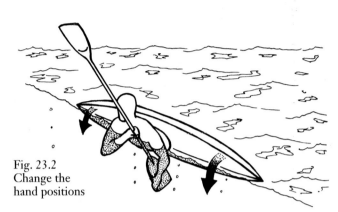

Fig. 23.2
Change the
hand positions

Fig. 23.3
Returning to the
surface

fish-eye view

Fig. 23.4
Finish with a
Hip Flick

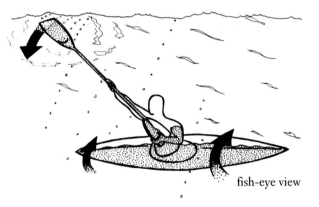

fish-eye view

3 Once you are completely upside-down, twist your body sideways and allow your shoulders to rise parallel to the surface. If you are in clear shallow water, the bottom should be directly facing you. Place the paddle shaft over your right shoulder so that the blade is sticking out in fresh air. The palm of your right hand is still facing outward. To raise yourself to the surface, strike the paddle down violently with your right hand (*see* fig. 23.3).

As the extended paddle strikes the water, lift the near blade with your left hand. As your body breaks the surface, perform a Hip Flick (*see* fig. 23.4).

Chapter 24 *Canadian Screw Roll*
(enclosed C1)

Mistakes are always best made in private. This unfortunate C1 paddler's capsize occurred in the presence of HRH The Princess Royal during the opening of Britain's new artificial slalom course at Nottingham.
PHOTO: TICKLE DESIGN GROUP

This roll is the most popular one with competitive C1 paddlers, both because of its speed and because the paddle finishes up with the driving face in position to continue the next forward paddling stroke.

The wind-up

The paddle is held in a similar manner as for the Screw Roll, except that the rear hand holds a T-bar. The blade is held parallel to the gunwale. The position of the T-grip hand is slightly to the rear of the hip. Lean well forward across the deck so that the outer edge of the paddle blade is angled down towards the surface of the water (*see* fig. 24.1).

Rolling method

1 Capsize in the direction indicated by the shaded arrow in figure 24.1. Once you are completely upside-down, lean your body up towards the light, at the same time pushing the paddle towards the surface (*see* fig. 24.1).

2 Keep the T-arm straight and sweep it out from the bow in an arc, maintaining the planing angle of the paddle blade and pulling violently downwards. At the same time flick your hips. This should bring you to the surface.

Your body will have followed the paddle round in its sweep. This is fine, so long as you keep your head and body low and near to the deck, towards the finish of the sweep. Remember that you are kneeling and there will be a lot of your body above the cockpit which has to be brought to the surface.

Even with the body kept low, you may still find difficulty in bringing off that final lift to the surface. If this is the case, allow the sweep of the paddle to go past the right-angle position in relation to the canoe (you might not in any case have a choice!). From this position, slightly towards the stern, rotate the wrists forward so that the knuckles face the water. Push down hard as the back of the blade planes forward and do a Hip Flick (*see* fig. 24.2). This should complete the roll.

Fig. 24.1
Movement diagram:
view from the rear

Fig. 24.2
Forward scull finish:
view from the front

CHAPTER 25 *Steyr Roll (C1)*

The wind-up

Hold the paddle in the normal paddling position. Place the paddle across your left shoulder, as shown in figure 25.1. The palm of the T-grip hand faces upwards as does the palm of the hand holding the shaft. Lean back as far as possible and capsize in the direction indicated by the arrow in figure 25.1.

Fig. 25.1
The wind-up

Rolling method

1 Once upside-down, your back should be touching the rear deck (*see* fig. 25.2). The knuckles of the 'shaft' hand should be next to your ear, with the blade pushed up towards the surface.

102

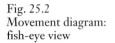

Fig. 25.2
Movement diagram:
fish-eye view

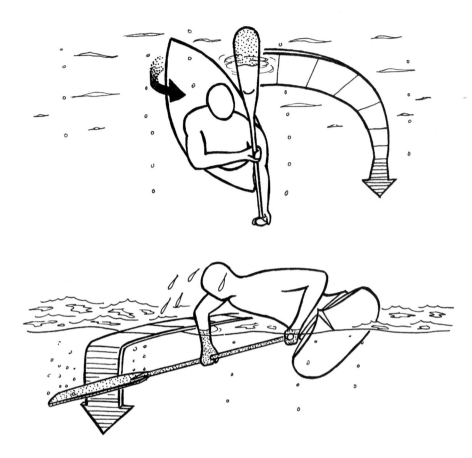

Fig. 25.3
Final downwards push

2 With the leading edge high, sweep the paddle blade outwards and forwards, at the same time keeping the T-bar hand near to the gunwale. Let your body follow the paddle out and round as it sweeps forward in an arc. Your body should stay parallel to the surface of the water (*see* fig. 25.3).

3 You should be starting to PUSH the paddle downwards and beginning the Hip Flick as the paddle reaches an angle of about 45° to the canoe. By the time the paddle gets at right angles to the canoe, the boat should be upright. Remember to keep the upper torso low and as near to the surface as possible during the final downward PUSH.

The Steyr Roll has the advantage of the strong leverage given by the length of the sweeping upper body added to that already afforded by the paddle. For this reason, many C1 paddlers prefer it to the Screw Roll.

CHAPTER 26 *Cross Bow Roll (C2)*

At this stage in the book the reader should immediately spot something rather strange about this method of rolling. The roll appears to be completely back-to-front. The wind-up begins with the paddle held comfortably (not usually the case) at the side of the canoe. As the roll continues, the hands and arms are crossed over the body in a very unnatural and excruciatingly awkward way. At the finish, the paddler is in a position of extreme instability and the boat could easily be on the verge of another capsize.

The Cross Bow cannot be described as a roll in its own right but only as a supporting roll executed at the same time as, and to complement, a roll done by a partner in a C2.

The only merit of the Cross Bow Roll lies in the fact that the paddler does not have to change sides to perform it. The advantage of this would be evident in a competition, where time used to change sides would be saved.

It is possible to use the Cross Bow Roll in a C1, but it is very difficult to be successful. It is more often used as a desperate Support Stroke to prevent an imminent capsize when in a downstream situation. It can also be used as a half roll on a river, when the paddle is placed into a stopper, again in a downstream situation, and the power of the water is used to bring the canoe upright.

The wind-up

Hold the paddle vertically in the normal paddling position on the paddling side, with the driving face looking inboard (*see* fig. 26.1). Lean well forward so that the T-bar hand is level with your shoulder. This will put the lower hand underwater.

Rolling method

1 You may capsize on either side. Once completely upside-down, make sure the paddle is still in the same position. It should now be sticking out of the water, vertically into the air.

2 To start the movement that will bring you to the surface, the shaft-hand is pushed firmly outwards. The T-bar hand will pull inwards. As it does so, the fingers and thumb must slacken sufficiently to allow the T-bar to rotate in the palm till the fingers and thumb have changed their position.

Fig. 26.1
The wind-up

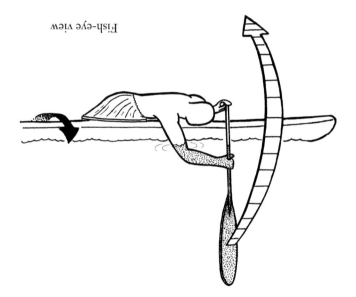

Fish-eye view

3 By the time the stroke is finished, the blade has moved from the vertical to the horizontal, parallel to the surface of the water. The T-bar hand is again gripping the T-bar, but now with the back of the hand coming in line with the back of the blade and the inner wrist in line with the driving face of the blade. It is in this position that you will feel the blade strike the surface of the water (*see* fig. 26.2).

4. Now is the time to push violently downwards. The T-bar hand will cross over to the other side of the body. At the same time, Hip Flick to the surface (*see* fig. 26.3).

As the roll finishes, you will be in a very vulnerable and unstable position. Until the canoe becomes stable once more, keep your body as low to the fore-deck as possible.

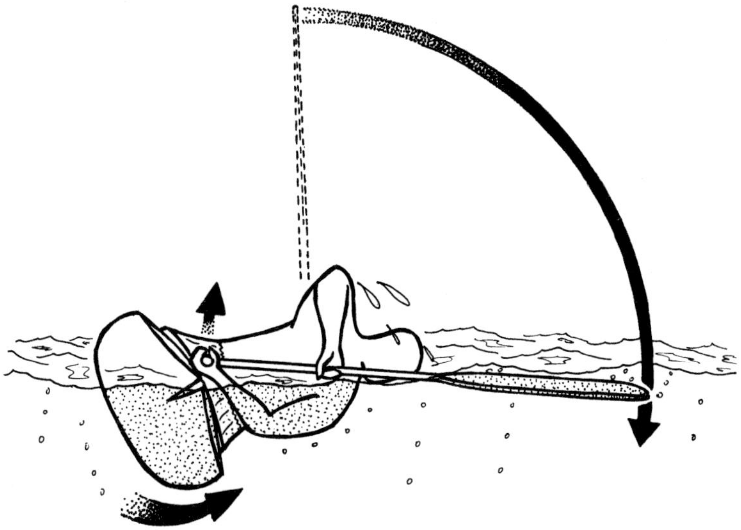

Fig. 26.2
Movement diagram:
view from the front

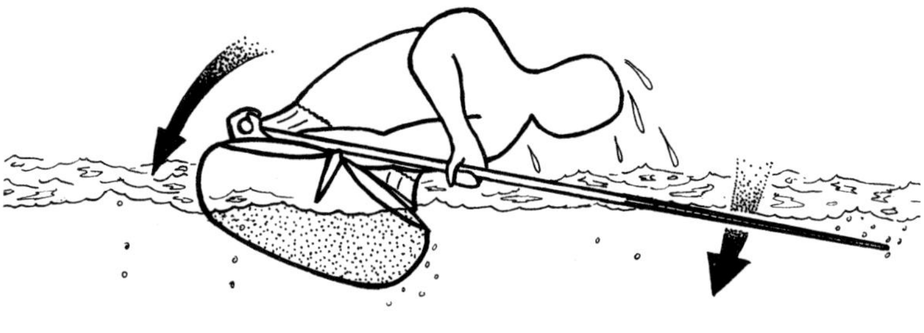

Fig. 26.3
Downward push and Hip
Flick: view from the front

Robin Witter *and his brother, Rodney, were British National C2 Champions in the early 1970s. Here Robin remembers their intriguing method of rolling a C2.*

The trouble with rolling a C2 is that you have to get things in sync. In the early days my brother and I had a novel method. We used a length of string! We got this 'string trick' from the Czechs, who were the best Canadian paddlers around at the time. One end of the string was tied to my big toe. The other end of the string went through the boat and was tied to Rodney's big toe.

You see, when you capsize in a C2 one man always has to change sides because he's been paddling on a different side to his partner. He has to take the time to get the paddle across to the other side before he can roll. Once in position the roll can begin. Of course if one man rolls too soon you're in trouble. So – I would change sides and when I was ready to roll I would give a pull on the string and then we'd both roll up together. Well, most times! We didn't tie the string too tight because it might have been awkward if we'd had to leave the boat.

Of course, as our technique improved, we progressed to one of us banging on the bottom of the hull to signal the start of the roll. One of us would bang on the bottom of the boat. You know – bang! one – bang! two – and roll up on the count of three.

During the time we'd progressed to the 'bang, bang', I remember we capsized in a big rapid. I waited ages for the signal . . . until I thought I was a goner . . . then eventually I came out – only to discover that my brother was already out. He had been out for ages! I suppose that was one good thing about the string!

This remarkable, award-winning photograph was taken during an attempt by Graeme Lowe to beat the world hand-rolling record. Unfortunately, things did not work out as well for the roller as they did for the cameraman. Graeme became disorientated and had to give up after forty-eight girations! PHOTO: MIKE COWLING, *The Northern Echo*

CHAPTER 27 *Hand Roll*

I had just started to draw the arrows on the movement diagram of the Hand Roll – and was musing that by now I must have drawn more arrows than Robin Hood and all his Merry Men put together – when my wife suddenly called out 'You must come and see this!'

The scene on the television screen was an all too familiar one. It was an indoor swimming pool and in the centre of the technicolour turquoise rectangle, a bright yellow kayak was being rolled over and over and over.

I gathered that a young man was attempting to break the world's hand-rolling record. Children and spectators in the balcony shouted and chanted encouragement. Down one side – up the other. Down one side – up the other! There seemed no pause either in the young man's

This young hand-roller rests his non-rolling hand on his spray-skirt. Kayaks designed for swimming pools are very easy to roll. With practice, you might find that you don't need to assist the roll with your upper hand. PHOTO: DEREK C. HUTCHINSON

rhythm or in his determination. Then the voice of the commentator interrupted to say that the record had been broken. Still the rotating kayak did not halt. The young man, whose body had gone into overdrive but whose brain was now locked into neutral, had to be physically stopped by friends and supporters who grabbed the boat to prevent any continuation of his agony.

When it was over, his comments were brief and breathless: 'I thought I might have done it when I was in training . . . I thought I was heading for 40 minutes . . . The canoe started to fill with water . . . I started to get pains around my chest and I was getting mentally discouraged . . . It was the crowds – they kept me going.' Colin Hill had just completed 1,000 Hand Rolls in 31 minutes 55 seconds!

Back in the early 1960s people spoke in hushed tones about those who, we had heard, could throw away their paddles and roll with only their hands. To us poor mortals, this was almost on a par with walking on the water. For the sake of posterity, I decided I would try and track down one of these gods of the Hand Roll. Who were these nameless few who started it all?

My luck was in, and I was able to contact Keith Wickham, now a successful businessman, whose main recreational participations are car and motor-cycle racing. But back in the swinging 1960s Keith's main interest was competing in kayak slalom. As he told me,

'I think I was probably one of the first people to perform a Hand Roll. I certainly hadn't heard of anyone else doing it before me. I remember in those days it was really only the slalomists who could roll at all and even then I know that some of the top men couldn't.

The Hand Roll was really the product of the Hip Flick – not the other way around. There was nobody to teach me to Hand Roll. I had to teach myself. I started by reaching down and touching the sand on the bottom with my fingers. Then I'd give a push and flick my hips. Once I got the kayak round, my body would follow. You see, a swimming pool would have been no good, because I wouldn't have been able to touch the bottom! It really was a circus piece! In fact, people used to gather around the dock to witness this "unbelievable" trick.

I went quickly from hand-rolling to one-hand-rolling. Eventually, I could do it with NO HANDS . . . I could just stick both hands down my spray-cover and roll the boat up with a flick of my head and upper body.'

In 1969 Keith Wickham became British Slalom Champion.

It is quite easy to teach yourself to Hand Roll using the following instructions. For convenience and safety's sake, however, it is a good idea to have a helper/instructor standing by to assist or at least to keep a watchful eye on your progress.

Land drill

You must first become familiar with the land drill as shown in figures 27.1 and 27.2. (This is assuming you wish to capsize on the left and roll up on the right.) The back of the right hand is facing the left ear, and the extended arm has its palm facing forwards.

Land drill

Fig. 27.1
Position from the front

Fig. 27.2
Movement diagram:
view from above

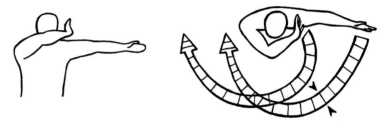

Fig. 27.1   Fig. 27.2

To get a better idea of what is happening, turn the movement diagram of figure 27.2 upside-down. Then imagine that you are upside-down and leaning back with your head touching the rear deck of your kayak. You are looking at the bottom of the pool or pond.

Start sweeping your straight left arm round. As your hand reaches the position indicated by the two pointers, start swinging round with your right hand. Your arms should be moving round with some violence, as if they are having a race. Your left hand will reach the right side a split second before the arrival of the right hand. Repeat the movement until it can be done smoothly, almost as second nature, one hand following slightly behind the other.

Remember that while you are doing all this, your head is supposed to be TOUCHING THE BACK DECK while you are looking straight down towards the bottom.

Learning with assistance

You are in shallow water. Adopt the starting position with your head touching the rear deck. The helper will reach underneath and lock fingers with you (*see* fig. 27.3). For this exercise keep your left arm by your side, out of the way. Capsize away from the helper who will allow his hand to bring yours round to his side.

   Wait until you are completely upside-down (*see* fig. 27.4). Then with a firm grip, pull down with your right hand. Upon rising to the surface (*see* fig. 27.5), the pupil must be told if the head was lifted even slightly

Fig. 27.3

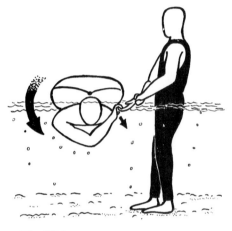

Fig. 27.4

Learning with assistance

Fig. 27.3
Assistant hooks student's
fingers from underneath

Fig. 27.4
The capsize:
student and assistant's
fingers are locked together;
the assistant supports their
wrist with the other hand

Fig. 27.5
The student rolls using
hand support

Fig. 27.5

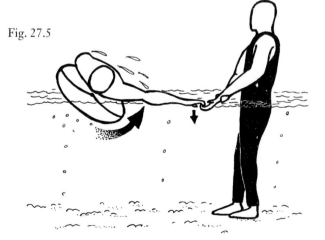

The finish of a Hand Roll. During this Hand Roll the upper hand is used for counter-balance to help bring the paddler round to the upright positio PHOTO: STEVE DORRITY

from the rear deck. This drill should now be done several times until the kayak can be hip-flicked round easily with only a slight pressure on the helper's hand and without any movement of the head from the deck.

During these exercises, I suggest that the helper gives some support to the wrist that is taking all the weight. Lifting the head is the kiss of death to a successful Hand Roll; it will also transform the student into a dead weight on the helper's now overstrained arm.

Without assistance

Some people find that they can move on to this stage immediately after learning the movement drill.

Position yourself near the side rail of a swimming pool or in water near to a point where you can swim the kayak into shallows and push upright. In order to progress to the unassisted Hand Roll you will need a couple of polystyrene swimming floats.

Lie back on the rear deck. Hold a float in each hand, ready on the left side. Now capsize. Twist your body round towards the rolling side,

Without assistance

Fig. 27.6
Using polystyrene
floats

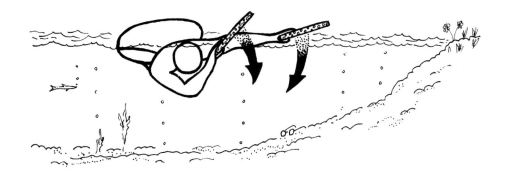

Fig. 27.7
Ready for the
Hip Flick

Fig. 27.8
The upper arm is
used as a counter-
balance to assist
righting

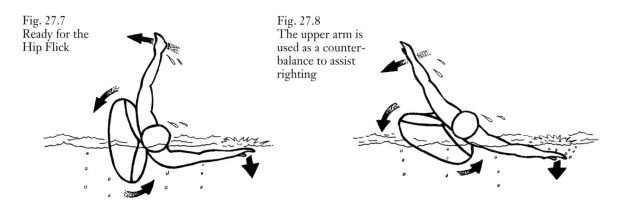

head towards the light (*see* fig. 27.6). Execute the now familiar
two-handed drill. So long as the head stays on the rear deck, you should
flick easily to the surface using the floats.

Repeat this exercise, reducing the size of the floats, and then discard
one; continue until you feel you can do without the other. When it
comes to using the hands only, keep your fingers slightly OPEN. This
will afford greater resistance to the water than if the fingers are held
close together. To give the boat added momentum at the moment of
Hip Flick (*see* fig. 27.7), as you come up, throw the upper arm over,
away from the roll side, as a counter-balance (*see* fig. 27.8).

CHAPTER 28 *Hooked Hand Roll*

This is called the Hooked Hand Roll because I couldn't think of any other name to distinguish it from the previous Hand Roll.

The wind-up

The hands are held like butterfly wings, with the thumbs hooked together and the fingers slightly parted (*see* fig. 28.1). The hands remain hooked together throughout the sweep. Practising this from left to right, you will notice that the left side and left shoulder have to twist over to allow the hands to arrive at the right side together.

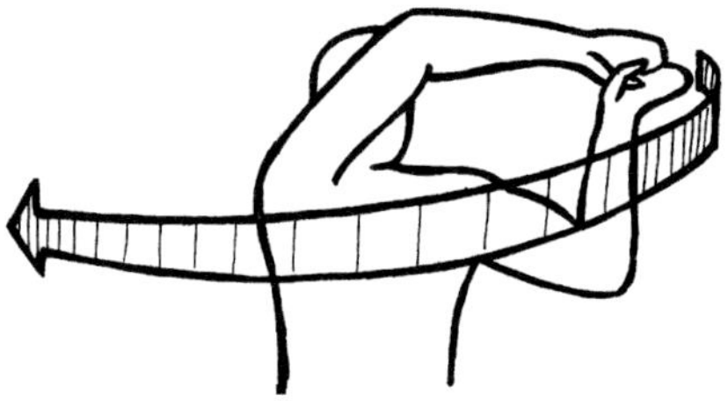

Fig. 28.1
Land drill movement diagram: view from the front

Rolling method

1 With the hands held as indicated, dive round into a capsize. As the body swings round, utilise the momentum and, as your body begins to swing towards the other side, push your arms and hands up towards the light and the surface.

2 As the hands meet the surface, reach out with your arms and pull the hands violently downwards.

3 As the kayak starts to rise, a final Hip Flick will bring you to the surface (*see* fig. 28.2, fish-eye view).

114

Fig. 28.2
The capsize position

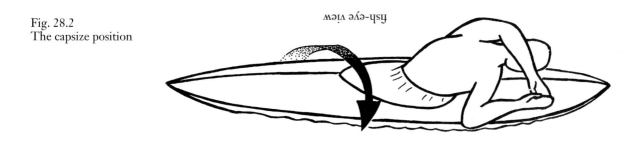

fish-eye view

Paul Newman, *BCU coach and a coaching organiser, provides an interesting story about students kayak rolling off the south coast of England.*

I was spending some time surfing with students from Leeds Polytechnic. There were quite a few wild big waves coming in and it wasn't long before I saw a chap get knocked down by a nasty, large wave – so he went into a roll. Unfortunately, he could only roll on one side – with the result that, instead of rolling up with the wave, he tried to roll up against the next one that came in – on the wrong side! Just as the wave picked him up to dump him, he did a pole vault. You see he was a big, powerful man and as he tried to roll he had the strength to keep hold of his paddle as the wave hit him. So he went over the top of his paddle. He literally did a pole vault on it. We saw the boat leave the water completely! Everybody stood and applauded this clever trick, until we realised that he didn't seem likely to reappear. We all dashed in and dragged him out. It was then we discovered that he'd dislocated his shoulder.

The local cottage hospital couldn't take him because it had no facilities for accident cases. We had to hold him together in a bumpy minibus in order to get him to the main hospital in Middlesbrough. We all waited in the corridor outside the operating theatre, where he'd been taken to have his shoulder put back in.

We noticed a steady stream of nurses and doctors going in, so we asked a nurse who came out, 'What's going on?' She replied, 'Well, we've got four holding him down, two pulling on his arm and another holding his legs – we've got bodies all over him!' It seemed that he was so well-muscled, they had great difficulty getting his shoulder back in again. Things eventually clicked into place, however, and he was soon as right as rain.

CHAPTER 29 *Re-entry and Roll*

This method of self-rescue is directed at those who paddle on the sea or large lakes. I personally would not advocate it on a white-water river.

The whole idea of the Re-entry and Roll is that it is possible to bail out of a kayak then get back in again upside-down and roll up. This is certainly not easy, and you will find that it requires skill and nerve. However, we are talking about calamities which require extreme remedies.

If you are paddling alone and get knocked out of your boat in rough water, make no mistake about it, you will be frightened. The first thing, therefore, is to calm down. If the water is cold it is important to get back into the kayak as quickly as possible. It is no good whatsoever rushing at this method of rescue like a headless chicken, but if you have practised Re-entry and Roll in a swimming pool then all should go well.

Method

1 Face the rear of the kayak, one arm stretched out underneath and holding on to the cockpit coaming on the far side (*see* fig. 29.1). Hold the paddle in the correct hand, ready for a roll on the side of your choice.

2 With both hands holding the coaming, steady the boat, take a deep breath and submerge. Still grasping the coaming and paddle, curl up your legs, drop your head back and let your legs enter the cockpit as part of a reverse somersault (*see* fig. 29.2). Some people are able to replace their spray-covers at this stage. Unfortunately, I am not one of them.

3 Once positioned firmly in the cockpit, now is the time to roll up.

You will discover that things can be much more difficult on open water than they are in a swimming pool. This is not only due to the temperature of the water or the roughness of the sea. It is also because

Fig. 29.1
Grasp the cockpit
and face the stern

Fig. 29.2
Swing the legs upwards

the shape of sea kayaks, together with buoyant clothing and a life-jacket make it almost impossible to actually get upside-down and into the starting position for the re-entry. The only thing to do is to just IGNORE the fact that you are not completely upside-down (as in fig. 29.3) and make all your movements exactly as you did in practice. Disregard the fact that water is breaking on your face and shoulders. Just remember that the method of re-entry is exactly the same . Do not be put off when you find yourself floating on the surface beside your kayak instead of looking at it from underneath.

Once upright and back in the boat your problems are not over. You will have to pump out or bail out as best you can. This is not an easy

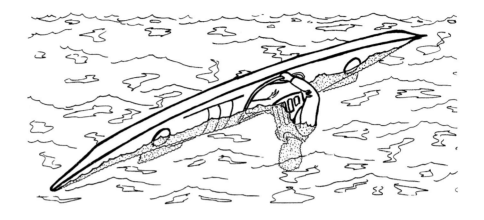

Fig. 29.3
Position of the paddler
wearing a life-jacket or
buoyancy aid during an
open water re-entry

task. The first time I tried this out at sea in some choppy water, it took me 15 minutes to empty the boat, during which time I felt nightmarishly unstable, and I found putting the spray-cover on was, to say the least, very awkward. At the end of the operation I felt thoroughly exhausted. The moral of the story is, of course: always kayak in company and remember that, once back in the kayak, you are back in the conditions which capsized you in the first place!

Mercia Sixta, *one of the first people in North America to gain the BCU's Senior Instructor's awards, is president of the Sea Kayaking Association of British Columbia. She describes her introduction to a Re-entry and Roll in the sea.*

We were off Point Atkinson. There was a slight chop on the water but nothing too great. We were practising strokes, rescues and rolling. During all this, I accidentally capsized. I started to go for a roll but I must have caught my paddle in my deck lines. It was my fault really because I'd been meaning to tighten these up. Anyhow, I had a couple of loose lines and my paddle got tangled in them. I managed to get rid of one of them, but I think I'd wrapped round one of the lines twice. The water was cold. It fairly took my breath away and I wasn't able to hold it very long. I know I got quite frightened. I wasn't going to be able to get free from the second one without coming up for air so I had to come out of the boat. Once in the water I managed to get the line untangled, then I did a Re-entry and Roll. I'd practised getting back into the boat upside-down and then rolling up, but I'd never done it for real outside a swimming pool. I remember when I finally rolled up, I got a nice round of applause from the others.

CHAPTER 30 *Rolling in rough water*

The last thing a competitor needs is to be forced into a roll during a competition when every second counts. No matter how fast the roll, too much time will be lost. Here a competitor has to roll his C1 Canadian during a Premier Division slalom competition on the River Tryweryn. The direction of the water plume from the paddler's head is an indication that he leaned well forwards at thebeginning of the roll. PHOTO: TICKLE DESIGN GROUP

Once you feel completely at home with your chosen roll, the time has come for you to go out and give it a try in the real world of rapids or surf. If your first practice area is to be on a river, choose a spot that is free from underwater obstructions, with not too fast a current. When you begin to feel confident, a few mild stoppers would be ideal. Go on to the smooth moving water first and experience the feeling of leaning upstream on the paddle. Notice how the water pushing your paddle under will capsize you. Then do the same thing, leaning downstream. Notice the support that the water can give you. Practise rolling over on the upstream side and use the water to assist you, when you roll up on the downstream side. Once you have the awareness that the movement of the water can get you to the surface, you will be able to apply the principle to much bigger rapids.

Under most conditions, it is important to roll as soon as possible after a capsize, otherwise you may be swept against rocks, under trees or

Fig. 30.1
Rolling in a stopper:
the paddler rolls up on
the downstream side

into even larger stoppers. However, while I advise speed, I do not advocate unseemly haste. Take the time to orientate yourself and get into the correct paddle position and stay calm enough to make the right paddle movement. Remember that you will waste far more energy in hasty, incorrect movements which lead to a fail roll than you would if you waited a few more seconds and did a successful one.

If you are upside-down and travelling downstream at the same speed as the surrounding flat water, you will find it does not matter which side you roll up on. If you are moving along upside-down through rapids, try to finish the final strike of the roll with your paddle on the downstream side. If you become caught in a stopper, roll up on the downstream side (*see* fig. 30.1). Even if you happen to be able to roll on only one side, you may find that all you have to do is to put the paddle out on the downstream side, then hang on and let the water do the rest. I have watched numerous people attempting to roll in stoppers, using so much force that they have thrown themselves over into yet another capsize.

Paddle breakage

Paddles do not break very often but when they do they usually snap at the neck or somewhere on the blade – which is where they get the most strain. If you are going for a roll and break a paddle you will become aware of the fact very quickly. All of a sudden there will be no resistance from the water against the paddle. The leverage you expected on the downward pull is just not there. Nor is that the only problem, for if, like me, you exhale on the downward pull, you will find yourself upside-down with empty lungs as well as a broken paddle.

If you are in the middle of a roll when your paddle snaps, allow yourself to fall back into the fully capsized position. *Turn the paddle round* so that you now have a good paddle blade at the working end. It may take you slightly longer to set the good blade at the correct angle, but it is time well spent.

An alternative method, for those who have completed the exercises for the Hand Roll, is as follows. Lean back on the rear deck and take hold of the broken paddle with the good blade in the hand next to your ear. Now use this as you would the polystyrene float.

A good exercise for those who paddle on the sea is to capsize and try rolling up using one half of the spare paddle from the rear deck. This is not easy and I would suggest that it is an exercise for sheltered waters or a swimming pool. It will also encourage you to adopt a sensible method of fastening your spare paddle, so that in an emergency it does not prove a purely ornamental and, alas, permanent fixture.

Cameron O'Connor, *one of America's leading women white-water paddlers, tells a story which is a thoughtful reminder that the elements should never be underestimated.*

I was paddling down the Tumwater Canyon in Washington State. It was big water – technical class 5+, with huge stoppers and big holes. I'd say it was running around 12,000 cubic feet per second. I was battling my way through these mountains of water when I dropped into a big hole and my spray-skirt came off. I tried to roll but it was quite difficult. I kept trying but it wasn't working. I'd always been able to roll so it didn't occur to me that I wouldn't be able to come up. I consciously made myself relax because I knew that I must concentrate. I thought, 'I'll try and roll up just one more time, then I'll bail out!' This last roll never materialised.

They found me upside-down at the bottom of a steep drop where the river turns into a lake. I was blue and I'd stopped breathing. I learned afterwards that I'd been underwater for about five minutes. I was revived by mouth-to-mouth resuscitation. When they found me, the paddle was still locked in my hand by a death grip.

They took me to hospital, but I was fine. I went paddling the following day. I had no bad after-effects except that for the next few weeks my memory was affected slightly. Little things – for instance, I couldn't remember telephone numbers that I'd always known.

CHAPTER 31 *Party tricks*

Changing kayaks underwater

This stunt always goes down well with audiences, especially if it is done in water which is not too clear, so that the underwater goings-on are concealed from the onlookers. To perform it successfully, the participants should be familiar with the Re-entry and Roll (*see* pp. 116–18).

You and a companion sit side by side about six to eight feet apart. To make things more interesting for the spectators, ask them to hold their breath too as you capsize. Secure your paddles to the kayak – an elasticated paddle park will be ideal for this. Capsize, vacate the cockpit, but keep hold of the cockpit coaming. Now push your head up into the cockpit space and get a lungful of air that will be trapped there. Now for the changeover. To make sure that you swim in the right direction, open your eyes. You should be able to see the shape of your companion looking in your direction. Swim towards the other boat. When you reach it push your head into its cockpit area and take another breath. Take your time as you re-enter and then roll up.

I remember the first time I ever did this with my friend Ron Miller. (Ron contributes a yarn elsewhere in this book.) The capsize and air-gulp went according to plan, but on the way to the other kayak I collided with Ron who was coming the opposite way. Disentangling ourselves must have created some turbulence because when I got to where the other boat should have been, it wasn't there! This was about the time I needed another gulp of air. I could make out the shape of his kayak about six feet or so farther on. I tried to keep calm and kept on swimming, until I was finally able to get a welcome breath of air from the air in the cockpit. I couldn't feel the paddle, where it should have been, next to the hull, so I had to pull my head down again and look around. Luckily the paddle was within reach so I grabbed it and rolled up. I came to the surface to a good round of applause and some rather bluish faces. Even Ron looked a little concerned.

'Dry hat' roll

The idea is to tell onlookers that you can capsize and roll up again without getting your hat wet (*see* Chris Hare's experience on p. 80). It is, of course, a trick – usually made easier if the hat has a brim or a large peak.

Suppose you are holding your hat in the left hand and the paddle in the right. Capsize on the paddle side, keeping the hat above the surface of the water as you go over. Once you are upside-down, lean forward, reach across and place the hat in your right hand. This hand will be holding the paddle blade in readiness for a Pawlata Roll. Once the hat is in position, bring the left arm back under the kayak and take hold of the paddle in the normal way and roll up. This trick can even be done with a lighted cigar. Unfortunately, cigarettes turn to mush in wet fingers.

An Eskimo Roll is no good unless it works when it counts. This photograph was taken at Bala Mill in Wales during the selection for the World Slalom Championships. Melvyn Jones was on his second run when he capsized at a critical stage in the event. He rolled up quickly and finished to win, thereby ensuring his place on the British Team. PHOTO: TICKLE DESIGN GROUP

Speed rolling

The aim of this masochistic exercise is to perform a set number of rolls, or Hand Rolls, as fast as possible. A thousand rolls seems to be the favourite number. I have already mentioned the hand-rolling record (*see* p. 108). The record for paddle-rolling goes to Ray Hudspeth who, with the support of cheering schoolchildren, completed one thousand Screw Rolls in 34 minutes 43 seconds – all done to raise money towards research into children's leukaemia.

At the end of this mind-boggling wet whizz-round, Ray remarked:

'I'm glad it's all over. I got cramp halfway through which slowed me down a bit.

I also lost my bathing cap, my nose-clip started to come off, and I got stuck against the side at one point – but I'm very pleased with the time. The kids were excellent. I think I've raised about £1,000.'

F. Spencer Chapman *was a member of the 1931 British Arctic Air Route Expedition. With Gino Watkins as their leader, the four main members of the expedition were among the first Europeans to live, paddle, and hunt with the Eskimos, using the indigenous sealskin-covered kayaks. Gino Watkins understood better than anyone how to handle and roll a kayak. He could roll using only the throwing stick. In spite of being fully aware of the dangers he also loved to go hunting alone. It was on one of these solo trips that he lost his life. It is believed he was killed by one of the huge waves generated by a calving glacier.*

The following extracts are from F. Spencer Chapman's book Watkins' Last Expedition.

The other day one of the hunters got an attack of kayak giddiness: this apparently only comes on in very still water and is probably caused by overmuch smoking. The victim told me that he became as it were hypnotised by the reflections in the water. He slowly capsized, recovering only when his head went underwater, and not sufficiently to enable him to come up unaided, though he was a competent roller. One, Iago, harpooned a bladder-nosed seal but failed to kill it. The animal attacked the kayak, and as often as the Eskimo came up again with his paddle the seal capsized him. At last he became too exhausted to roll any longer, so wriggled out of his kayak and held on to the float. The seal then wound the hunting-line round him and bit one of his boots off; but Iago managed to get out his pocket-knife and cut the line, after which the seal had the decency to make off.

There was a really big swell coming back across Angmagssalik Fiord and we had to put our kayak coats on. I was very unsteady; the trouble in a big sea is that I have to spend so much time balancing with the paddle that I don't keep enough headway. Today there were bunches of seaweed about and whenever my paddle caught in one I all but capsized. In the evening I tried rolling in a very rough sea. Wearing a kayak coat and being prepared to roll makes all the difference and I felt perfectly happy in the roughest water. It is very much easier to roll if you go over with the wind and let it help you up again. Much less effort is needed if you start to come up again before the kayak has come to a standstill on its way over. I managed to roll in eight different ways with the paddle, then for the first time I came up with my hand alone. By the end of the day I learnt to roll with left or right hand, both by the forward and backward methods. There are several ways of rolling with the paddle which I am sure I could never learn however long I practised, especially the methods when you start off with the paddle behind the neck, and the one when you keep the paddle underneath the kayak all the time.

Some time ago the schoolmaster here, who is an indifferent hunter but a very skilful roller, shot too far out to the side with his shotgun, and capsized. Before coming up again he had the presence of mind to push the gun back into the seal-skin cover on the deck of the kayak: he was quite annoyed that his pipe had gone out!

When you are paddling a kayak you keep on passing the paddle to and fro in your hands so that as much of the blade as possible is underwater at each stroke. My gloves were brand new and had been copiously soaked in blubber to make them waterproof. This made them very sticky, and as I passed the paddle through my hands it would sometimes stick, thus breaking the rhythm of the motion and almost upsetting me. Once this happened at the same moment as a wave hit me, and before I had time to do anything about it I was upside-down. I came up again at once, without much difficulty, using the Storm Roll which brings one up in a steady position.

The natives say there is no danger of the kayak being damaged unless the waves actually break against the chest of the man. In parts of the extreme south of Greenland, they are more used to kayaking in rough seas; when they see an exceptionally dangerous wave coming they capsize on purpose, take the wave on the bottom of the kayak instead of letting it hit them in the chest, and then when the wave is safely past they come up again with the paddle. In this district they can also go over end-ways-on in the kayak, using a big wave to carry them over backwards, after which they come up again in the ordinary way. The great thing if you capsize in a big sea is not to drop your paddle. If two men only are there and one drops his paddle, after he has been helped up nothing can be done because the rescued man cannot be left without support, and in a stormy sea the two together cannot catch up with the paddle. Several lives have been lost in this way.

Conclusion

In the extract from F. Spencer Chapman's book (see pp. 124–5) he mentions a roll done with the paddle behind the neck. I had never seen such a roll, so couldn't describe it.

As luck would have it, though, in the spring of 1987 I was visiting my son and his family in Guernsey. A friend phoned to say he had a video of an ancient cine film that he thought would interest me. He only had to mention that it was of Gino Watkins and I was round at his house like a shot.

It was in fact a film of a Gino Watkins' expedition among the Eskimos, and it was full of fascinating shots of Watkins and his team learning how to roll by copying them. They learned pretty well, even if they did provide some entertainment for the Eskimos, who obviously found their awkwardness hilarious. Suddenly, in the flickering film, there was an Eskimo performing a most unusual roll. It was over in seconds but this, I thought with excitement, was *the* roll described by Spencer Chapman and possibly even one of the methods described by David Crantz 200 years before Chapman. On that evening, and on

Greenland Trick Roll

Fig. A
Movement diagram

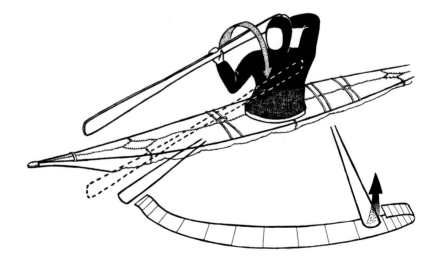

**Greenland Trick Roll,
continued**

Fig. B
Recovery position

several occasions since, I watched and rewatched, frame by frame, that swiftly executed roll. Three things are quite certain: the Eskimo goes over on his left; he comes up on his right (*see* figs. A and B); on becoming upright he brings the paddle over his head from behind his neck. The rest of the movement remains a dark, flickering uncertainty.

At first it appeared that the leading hand going over was his left hand, but when he came up, it was definitely his right. There was a dim suggestion of two sweeps of the paddle underwater. Was the Eskimo having his own fun and changing hands while upside-down? There hardly seemed to be time for that. Finally, after many eye-straining attempts to work out just what his wind-up position was, I have tried to draw what I think he was doing. Yes, I think he WAS having his bit of fun, but simply by putting the paddle behind his head. In this way, he was deliberately baffling the spectators by diverting their attention and making them assume the paddle changed sides. At least, I THINK that's what he was doing. If any readers know better, I'd be glad to hear from them.   If all this proves nothing else, it shows at least that in the art of Eskimo Rolling, all is not yet mastered. There are always the rumours of yet one more roll, other trails to follow and other fascinating stories to track down.

A last word

Richard Fox *is the world's foremost white-water slalom paddler. He is a four-time world champion, the 1992 World Cup champion, and has won two world championships in team competition. Here Richard remembers a roll in the heat of competition and two televised rolling contests, then parts with a word of advice.*

Rarely have I had to roll up during a race, and the only time I have had to do it on both runs was in Tasmania during March 1992. It was a World Cup race on big water, about Grade IV, I would say the biggest we've raced on. On my first run I got down all the gates cleanly until gate 20, a difficult one with a boiling eddyline with whirlpools running down it. On this upstream gate it was hard to judge the entry into the eddy that would place me in the middle of the gate. I eddied out too soon, and had to lean back just to get my head through the gate, which threw me off balance. I went through the gate alright but with too much speed, and my momentum seemed to spin me out too soon. After that I lost control completely and suddenly I was over!

I think I did more of a power flip than a roll. I came up quickly, and still managed to ferry across the jet of rushing water to the next gate, but I was totally disoriented. Somehow, I don't know how, I held it together and got through the last three gates. The whole business had cost me at least a couple of seconds but to my delight I still ended up second!

The lesson to be learned is that even if you're racing and things go wrong, with a quick roll you can pick it up and keep going to finish the course.

I once accepted a friendly challenge from a 'Mr Average Canoeist' in Holland, to see which of us could do more rolls in one minute. On the appointed day, the organisers began by telling me I was not allowed to practise and said, 'Oh, and sorry, but there's no heating in the pool!' I thought no more about it – after all, it was just a friendly bout. We waited and waited and eventually discovered, just before the event, that this was going out on live TV. Then we were ON!

The water was absolutely FREEZING. It turned out to be frightening because when you're not used to it, you get very dizzy, going over and over. I can remember getting to 15 or so and then just struggling dazedly through a few more and I eventually managed 22. But I was beaten by the local boy, who did 23. I like to think it was because he'd been practising religiously for weeks and had a short, round boat whereas I had a slalom. Nevertheless, I felt a bit embarrassed being beaten publicly.

In 1987 I again accepted the challenge, this time on a British TV programme called 'You Bet'. This one was more fun. The water was warm. There was a big studio audience to cheer us on and I was allowed to practise briefly beforehand. But the big difference was that I knew what to expect. I took it at a steadier pace and kept the rhythm going right through. I managed 25, but the young, English challenger, a local boy from the London area, looked as though he was going to match me. But the clock stopped him at 24½, so I just pipped him. The thing is, people like me make a career of trying to stay upright, so when it comes to rolling contests, we tend to be out of practice.

Rolling should be instinctive. Learn to roll left hand and right hand, with and without the paddle, upstream and downstream, and so on, so that as you get better you need to rely on your roll less and less.

Practise in realistic situations on rivers. Practise rolling in a stopper where you know that if you don't make it you can swim to shore. The same in the sea – practise your skills in the surf. Get to a stage where you're not afraid to be upside-down. A lot of things can go wrong, but surprisingly there are very few accidents.

Learn to relax. If you do go over, it's usually sudden and unexpected. The people that come off the best in the biggest water and the most dangerous situations are able to consider the situation with relative calm. It should all come automatically, but in a controlled way. Survivors and winners don't panic – they control themselves and take the appropriate action.

APPENDIX *Customising your seat position*

The first edition of this book suggested that a narrow piece of wood pushed across the knees or legs and wedged under the cockpit coaming would provide better support for rolling. Hindsight is a wonderful thing, and I've thought better of the suggestion. Following are a few other methods I have found effective over the years. Some involve using fibreglass. Those to whom this substance is a mystery would do well to read Joe Matuska's article in *Sea Kayaker*, 'Fiberglass Repairs' (Vol. 1, No. 3, Winter 1984, page 31). Reprints are available on request from *Sea Kayaker*.

In the following instructions I refer to fibreglass as GRP (glass-reinforced plastic). The descriptions are not meant to constitute step-by-step instructions. Rather, they are ideas with options, depending upon whether your boat is made of plastic or GRP. Experimentation may be necessary – but you'll enjoy it all!

Fig. A1
Foam block build-up. The finished work can be cut to fit the legs by using a hacksaw blade. Note thigh padding and back-strap

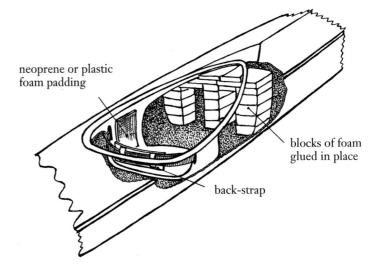

neoprene or plastic foam padding

blocks of foam glued in place

back-strap

Fig. A2
The knee tube provides a
dual function. It gives storage
space as well as support for
the knees when rolling

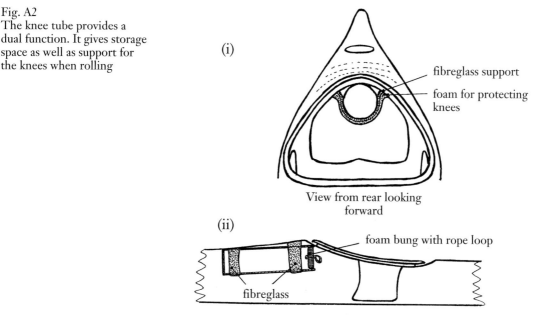

(i)

fibreglass support

foam for protecting
knees

View from rear looking
forward

(ii)

foam bung with rope loop

fibreglass

View from the side

Before installing any system of knee support, you need to make sure your posterior fits snugly in the seat with no sideways movement. This can be done by gluing neoprene or thin Ensulite foam (the rolled-up stuff that backpackers sleep on) to both sides of the seat (*see* fig. A1). When you push on the footrest, you should not slide backwards, so if the kayak has no back support, make one or fit a back-strap.

If you have no fibreglass skills or don't want to drill holes in your new kayak, I suggest the foam block build-up method for knee and leg support (*see* fig. A1). Glue blocks of closed-cell foam into position with impact adhesive. Using a hacksaw blade, cut the whole affair to fit to allow easy entry and exit, and then round it off. For a professional look, cover the blocks with thin foam, carefully cut and glued on to the surface.

My favourite method is the knee tube (*see* fig. A2). The idea is to 'lay up' GRP around a piece of 4-inch pipe. In other words, stipple liquid resin into glass matt that is wrapped around the pipe. Once the resin has set hard, slide the pipe out leaving a lightweight GRP tube. Before moulding, I find it helpful to put a saw cut all the way down the pipe. This makes releasing it from the finished GRP tube much easier. You might also wax the pipe to further abet its eventual release.

Make your tube about 15 inches long, and seal the far end with a cut circle of foam glued in place with impact adhesive. Suspend your kayak upside-down from a couple of ropes in your garage or workshop. Hold the GRP tube temporarily in place with duct tape (*see* fig. A2 (i)) and glass it in permanently with two strips of glass matt, say 2–3 inches wide, already wetted with resin (*see* fig. A2 (ii)). Once the tube is in position, make a 2-inch thick foam bung for the entrance and use thin Ensulite or Ethafoam to cover all surfaces of the tube and deck where your knees will touch.

The joy of the knee tube is that it not only gives excellent support during rolling or bracing but also provides locker space for those little niceties such as sunscreen, sunglasses, camera, and spare film.

I see no reason why a GRP knee tube could not be fitted to a plastic kayak using aluminium straps about 2 inches wide and ⅛ inch thick. The straps would be fastened to the deck with stainless steel dome-headed nuts and bolts. The thin foam padding would protect the paddler from the uneven screw heads.

GRP kayaks may also be fitted with wooden knee bars (*see* fig. A3). Slightly rounded or oval bars are comfortable and are glassed in place as shown. A more professional finish can be achieved by making the bars from two lengths cut from an old aluminium paddle shaft. These can be flattened at the ends and glassed neatly into place. If the ends were flattened at right angles to each other (feathered), it would be possible to fix the rear end of the bar to the inside surface of the seat upright. These aluminium bars could also be used in a plastic kayak, but it would mean drilling the boat and fixing the bars with dome-headed, stainless steel nuts and bolts.

Fig. A3
Large cockpit – GRP kayak

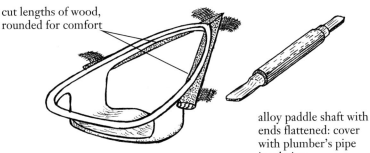

cut lengths of wood, rounded for comfort

alloy paddle shaft with ends flattened: cover with plumber's pipe insulation

Fig. A4
Knee braces made from
fibreglass (GRP). These can
be fitted to a GRP kayak or
one made from plastic

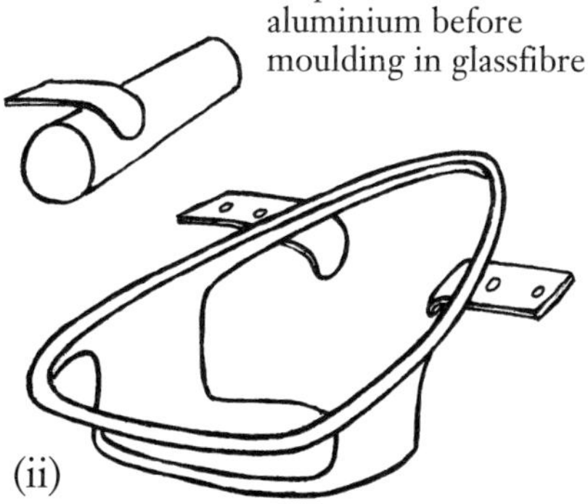

Fig. A5
Knee brace for GRP kayak
with a small cockpit but a
steeply sloping fore-deck

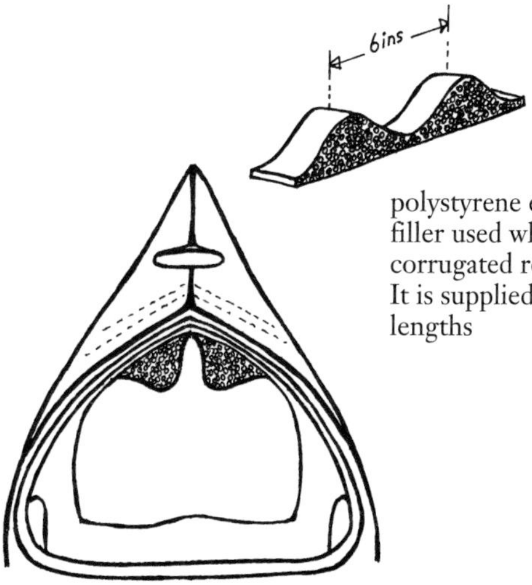

use 4-inch plumber's
pipe as a former to
shape a knee brace in
aluminium before
moulding in glassfibre

(i)

(ii)

6ins

polystyrene end-space
filler used when fixing
corrugated roofs.
It is supplied in
lengths

View from rear looking forward

It is not difficult to make knee braces from GRP. These can be fixed into a GRP kayak or one made from plastic (*see* fig. A4 (ii)). With a hide or rubber mallet, shape a piece of aluminium about 3–4 inches wide and about a foot long over a piece of 4-inch PVC pipe into a curve that will fit your thighs (*see* fig. A4 (i)). Use this aluminium shape as the form upon which to lay up the GRP. The finished knee braces can be glassed in place in a GRP kayak or drilled and fitted to a plastic kayak with stainless steel dome-headed nuts and bolts.

Some small cockpits present special problems. Kayaks with steeply pitched fore-decks tend to force the knees to slide together towards the centreline of the deck, thus losing the vital grip (*see* fig. A5). The polystyrene end-space filler used when fixing corrugated roofs can be used as a support to hold the knees apart. These fillers come in various lengths and sizes depending on the width of the roof sheets and the size of the corrugations. I find the filler measuring 6 inches between corrugation 'peaks' is best. Cut a 'two-bump' piece from the strip, bend slightly, and glue in place with contact adhesive for excellent results.

Index